Pandemic Pandemonium

A world in Conflict

Other Works by Myrna Skoller

Miracle on 81st Street: Designer Resale a Girl's Dream

Private Lessons With Jesus

Letters to Heaven and Back: A Journey Into Self-Healing

I Remember Grandpa

Sydney Goes to Bat

Pandemic Pandemonium

A World in Conflict

Myrna Skoller

PANDEMIC PANDEMONIUM—A WORLD IN CONFLICT All rights reserved. No part of this book may be reproduced or transmitted in any form or by any means, electronic or otherwise, including photocopying, without express written consent of the author.

Copyright ©2022
Myrna J. Skoller

Published by:
Soul Search Publications
soulsearchpublications@gmail.com

Book design by:
Jay R. Pizer
Imax Productions
www.imaxproductions.com

Publisher's Cataloging-in-Publication data:
Skoller, Myrna. J.
Pandemic Pandemonium—A world in Conflict
ISBN 978-1-7369594-6-6

Foreward

This is a time of repose for so many. The world was tired of staying locked up and so there were breakouts occurring everywhere in the world. Thousands upon thousands of people are once again joining together even though there are those who say it isn't over. Yet the ones who should be celebrating with us are instead continuing to give us fear. And this all pertains to the bad habits of the media whose only goal is to market their products. But there are those of us who can see through these cracks and even some watching the news are becoming aware of the games they play, and the game is to keep us watching at any cost.

Formerly, our unemployment rate in this country was astronomical as millions had lost their jobs. We are now regaining our footing as the unemployment rate has lowered.

At first, they told us to stay home and not go out and then they frightened us with news of low employment and a destroyed economy. They didn't say "temporary unemployment," they didn't say "unemployment before recovery." They told us we were doomed unless we adhered to what they were saying and did not care if what they told us was true or not. This, in fact, still holds true, because that is the habit of the media. We do not need to live in the fear which is forced upon us just so that they can sell their products. We just need to see things as they truly are.

Yet no matter what is said regarding serious research or solid reasoning, those who are glued to their TV sets are not necessarily willing to change. What is more dangerous than anything else, is passivity. An objective person doubts and relies on truth in order to advance and does not rely on ready-made answers which pop up every minute, of every hour, of every day. Yet no paper, no scientist, and no reasonable explanations will ever change the minds of those who have already been convinced. Any contradictory information to what they are told and choose to believe is passed off as fake news and disinformation. Those are the blind-faith believers who are steadfast in discounting the opinions of those in opposition.

In searching for news outside the confines of mainstream media, I have found a wealth of new information. I am blown away by how many world-renowned professionals from all walks of life, whether they be doctors, economists, scientists, microbiologists, virologists, epidemiologists and the like, who are willing to come forward and speak their truth, only to be censored time and time again. These professionals are the heart and soul of this book which is based on their opinions. I very much wanted to venture outside the confines of mainstream news so I did some serious searching. What I found was newsworthy information pouring in from all corners of the world. There is an infinite amount of information readily available on the subject of the pandemic if we just look to find it. Actually, I could write volumes based on all the information that is available, but this book must end somewhere. Still, there is so much more waiting to be discovered.

Preface

The book you are about to read is comprised of news articles from various different sources, some of which paint pictures of a world mired in corruption because of the unsavory practices of our local politicians, Big Pharma, governments and the media. We can indeed create change if we rise above the lies telling us that chaos is front and center of all that is happening and nothing else. When we seek to make this world a happier one, we have God's blessing. And then... and then... nothing is impossible. We can certainly help the process by being the best we can be, as kind, caring and compassionate beings.

When enough people join together in this way, we find that there is a far better world waiting to show itself. However, the media promotes false beliefs which in itself creates fear. Absent fear, we need not be limited as the media persists in conditioning us to believe these great distortions of truth. If we believe we are helpless victims, then we are indeed powerless to create change.

There are so many sources outside of mainstream media which gives us a different view of things. We can't always know what is true, but we can always know what feels to be true and relying on our own inner wisdom is sometimes the best source of truth. At least by venturing outside of the mainstream, we get other viewpoints and thus draw our own conclusions from that. So much of what is true is censored and suppressed by the media.

When we can rely on the good nature of those who want to make this a better and a safer place, not only for the entirety of the nation but for the world, then change will come about more rapidly than we might anticipate. Nonetheless, this is a realistic endeavor because they are the ones who will tell us the truth and fight for our freedoms. If enough of us learn to practice love, kindness and compassion, then the world will change accordingly. Love overcomes fear and has the power to change the world to one of peace, does exist. We just need to find those leaders who can, and will, make it happen.

I truly believe the world is waking up to a newer and better reality and once that happens, we can only venture forward. What will change the world is when we are no longer willing to yield to the misguided wishes of the few and start relying on the Herculean strength of the many. Joined together we can move mountains. Only then will we go up the ladder to a greater and more fulfilling reality. Believe it or not, it is already happening - the scales are tipping. Larger and larger groups of people are beginning to wake up to the reality of what is truly happening all around the world.

Understanding that peace is also happiness, is a giant leap towards achieving it. Above all, we deserve to be happy. Understanding that peace cannot co-exist with fear lies the recognition that we have taken another giant step forward.

No one has the power to deprive us of our rights to peace, least of all the media if we do not invest so heavily in it.

Introduction

The coronavirus is garnering the attention of the entire world. We had been locked in isolation for long periods of time and the news was, and continues to be, causing great fear in so many. We were not told that malaria, typhoid, HIV and other epidemics caused the death tolls to be much higher. Because the numbers are so much lower than that of previous diseases, it does not warrant these severe types of restrictions.

We have all been transformed in one way or another because of this global lockdown. For this reason, there is always a constant thrust of fear being forced upon us while businesses have collapsed, and the economy has suffered. Those in global control use their powers to keep entire countries in isolation in order to gain control over the entire population.

These control measures were put in place so that we are not challenging governments and people are much easier to control. We were convinced that to gather with others was life threatening. This is a very clever strategy. We are much more manageable as a population if we believe that going outside and talking to people is going to kill us.

This is a time to reflect and use our consciousness in sync with the transformations taking place so that we will be prepared and not fearful. Our freedoms have been curtailed in many ways. Yet this does not mean we need to be quaking in our shoes either. We need instead to use those restrictions to our own benefit by being more loving, creative and productive.

Instead of wasting our time in fear, it is far better to focus on the transformation which is now taking place which can actually enrich us mentally, emotionally and spiritually if we remain strong. One thing that can never be defiled is freedom of the mind, which is so much greater than freedom of the body.

Chapter 1

"The pharmaceutical industry is unique in that all large pharmaceutical firms explicitly state that they are focused on promoting patient welfare, yet the majority of large pharmaceutical companies engage in illegal activities that harm patient welfare," said Denis G. Arnold, a coauthor of the study and a professor at the University of North Carolina in Charlotte.

Jusitice department announces largest healthcare fraud settlement in its history

American pharmaceutical giant Pfizer Inc. and its subsidiary Pharmacia & Upjohn Company Inc. have agreed to pay $2.3 billion, the largest health care fraud settlement in the history of the Department of Justice, to resolve a civil liability arising from the illegal promotion of certain pharmaceutical products, the Justice Department announced.

Four U.S. Companies will pay $26 billion to settle claims that fueled the opiod crisis

Four of the largest U.S. Corporations have agreed to pay roughly $26 billion to settle a tsunami of lawsuits linked to claims that their business practices helped fuel the deadly opioid crisis. Johnson & Johnson, the consumer products and health giant that manufactured generic opioid medications will contribute $5 billion to the settlement.

MYRNA SKOLLER

You can't sue Pfizer or Moderna if you have severe COVID vaccine side effects. The government likely won't compensate you for damages either

If you experience severe side effects after getting a COVID vaccine, lawyers tell CNBC there is basically no one to blame in a U.S. court of law.

The federal government has granted companies like Pfizer and Moderna immunity from liability if something unintentionally goes wrong with their vaccines.

"It is very rare for a blanket immunity law to be passed" said Rogge Dunn, a Dallas labor and employment attorney. You also can't sue the Food and Drug Administration for authorizing a vaccine for emergency use, nor can you hold your employer accountable if they mandate inoculation as a condition of employment.

Congress created a fund specifically to help cover lost wages and out-of-pocket medical expenses for people who have been irreparably harmed by a "covered countermeasure," such as a vaccine. But it is difficult to use and rarely pays. Attorneys say it has compensated less than 6% of the claims filed in the last decade.

Immune to lawsuits

In February, Health and Human Services secretary Alex Azar invoked the Public Readiness and Emergency Preparedness Act. The 2005 law empowers the HHS secretary to provide legal protection to companies making or distributing critical medical supplies, such as vaccines and treatments, unless there's "willful misconduct by the company. The protection lasts until 2024.

That means that for the next two years, these companies "cannot be sued for money damages in court" over injuries related to the administration or use of products to treat or protect against COVID.

HHS declined CNBC's request for an interview.

PANDEMIC PANDEMONIUM

Dunn thinks a big reason for the unprecedented protection has to do with the expedited timeline.

"When the government said, 'We want you to develop this four or five times faster than you usually do,' most likely the manufacturers said to the government, we want you, the government, to protect us from multimillion-dollar lawsuits" said Dunn.

It's very rare for a blanket immunity law to be passed ...Pharmaceutical companies typically aren't offered much liability protection under the law

The quickest vaccine ever developed was for mumps. It took four years and was licensed in 1967. Pfizer's COVID-19 vaccine was developed and cleared for emergency use in eight months—a fact that has fueled public mistrust of the Coronavirus inoculation in the U.S.

Roughly 4 in 10 Americans say they would "definitely" or "probably" not get vaccinated, according to a recent survey by the Pew Research Center. While this is lower than it was two months ago, it still points to a huge trust gap.

But drug makers like Pfizer continue to reassure the public no shortcuts were taken. "This is a vaccine that was developed without cutting corners," CEO Dr. Albert Bourla said in an interview with CNBC's "Squawk Box" on Monday. "This is a vaccine that is getting approved by all authorities in the world. That should say something."

The legal immunity granted to pharmaceutical companies doesn't just guard them against lawsuits. Dunn said it helps lower the cost of immunizations.

"The government doesn't want people suing the companies making the COVID vaccine. Because then, the manufacturers would probably charge the government a higher price per person per dose," Dunn explained.

Pfizer and Moderna did not return CNBC's request for comment on their legal protections.

Is anyone liable?

Remember, vaccine manufacturers aren't the ones approving their product for mass distribution. That's the job of the FDA.

Which begs the question, can you sue the U.S. government if you have an extraordinarily bad reaction to a vaccine?

Again, the answer is no.

"You can't sue the FDA for approving or disapproving a drug," said Dorit Reiss, a professor at the University of California Hastings College of Law. "That's part of its sovereign immunity."

There are limited exceptions, but Dunn said he didn't think they provide a viable legal path to hold the federal government responsible for a COVID vaccine injury.

Bringing workers back to the office in a post- COVID world also carries with it a heightened fear of liability for its employers. Lawyers across the country say their corporate clients are reaching out to them to ask whether they can require employees to get immunized.

Dunn's clients who run businesses serving customers in person or on site are most interested in mandating a COVID vaccine for staff.

"They view it as a selling point," Dunn said. "It's particularly important for restaurants, bars, gyms and salons. My clients in that segment of the service industry are looking hard at making it mandatory, as a sales point to their customers."

While this is in part a public relations tactic, it is legally within an employer's rights to impose such a requirement.

"Requiring a vaccine is a health and safety work rule, and employers can do that," said Reiss.

There are a few notable exceptions. If a work force is unionized, the collective bargaining agreement may require negotiating with the union before mandating a vaccine.

Anti-discrimination laws provide some protections as well. Under the Americans With Disabilities Act, workers who don't want to be vaccinated for medical reasons are eligible to request an exemption. If taking a vaccine is a violation of a "sincerely held" religious belief, Title VII of the Civil Rights Act of 1964 would potentially provide a way to opt out.

Should none of these exemptions apply, employees may have some legal recourse if they suffer debilitating side effects following a work-mandated COVID inoculation.

Attorneys say claims would most likely be routed through worker's compensation programs and treated as an on-the-job injury.

"But there are significant limits for the caps of damages an employee can recover," said Dunn. He added that it would be likely difficult to prove.

Mandatory vaccination protocols, however, may not happen until the FDA formally approves the vaccines and grants Pfizer and BioNTech or Moderna a license to sell them, which will take several more months of data to show their safety and effectiveness.

"An Emergency use authorization is not a license," said Reiss. "There's a legal question as to whether you can mandate an emergency observation. The language in the act is somewhat unclear on that."

$50,000 a year

The government has created a way for people to recover some damages should something go wrong following immunization.

In addition to the legal immunity, the PREP Act established the Countermeasures Injury Compensation Program (CICP), which provides benefits to eligible individuals who suffer serious injury from one of the protected companies.

The little-known government program has been around for a decade, and it is managed by an agency under HHS. (U.S. Department of Health and Human Services) This fund typically only deals with vaccines you probably would never get, like the H1N1 and anthrax vaccines.

If a case for compensation through the CICP (Countermeasures Injury Compensation Program) is successful, the program provides up to $50,000 a year in unreimbursed lost wages and out-of-pocketed medical expenses. It won't cover legal fees or anything to compensate for pain and suffering.

It is also capped as a death benefit of $370,376, which is the most a surviving family member receives in an event that a COVID vaccine proves to be fatal.

But experts specializing in vaccine law say it is difficult to navigate. "This government compensation program is very hard to use," said Reiss. "The bar for compensation is very high."

Also worrisome to some vaccine injury lawyers is the fact that the CICP has rejected a majority of the compensation requests made since the program began 10 years ago. But of the 449 claims filed, the CICP has compensated only 29 claims, totaling more than $6 million.

People who are harmed by a covid vaccine deserve to be compensated fast and generously—the prep act doesn't do that

David Carney, vice president of the Vaccine Bar Association, said the CICP might deny a claim for a variety of reasons. "One reason might be that the medical records don't support a claim," said Carney, who regularly deals with vaccine injury cases. "We have to litigate a lot of really complex issues... and provide a medical basis for why the injury occurred."

Proving an injury as a direct result of the COVID vaccine could be difficult, according to Carney. "It's not as simple as saying 'Hey I got a COVID treatment and now I have an injury.' There is a lot of burden of proof there."

PANDEMIC PANDEMONIUM

There is also a strict one-year statute, meaning that all claims have to be filed within 12 months of receiving the vaccine.

"People are harmed by a COVID vaccine deserve to be compensated fast and generously," said Reiss. "The PREP Act doesn't do that."

Lawyers tell CNBC that it would make more sense for COVID vaccine injuries to instead be routed through another program under the HHS called the National Vaccine Injury Compensation Program, which handles claims for 16 routine vaccines. Known colloquially as "vaccine court," the program paid about 70% of petitions adjudicated by the court from 2006 to 2018.

And since it began considering claims in 1988, the VICP (Vaccine Injury Compensation Program) has paid approximately $4.4 billion in total compensation. That dwarfs the CICP's roughly $6 million in paid benefits over the life of the program.

The VICP also gives you more time to file your claim. You have three years from the date of the first symptom to file for compensation.

"The VICP allows for recovery of pain and suffering, attorney's fees, along with medical expenses and lost wages, if any," said Michael Maxwell, a lawyer who practices in the areas of business litigation and personal injury. "Under CIPC, it's only lost wages and out-of-pocket medical expenses. That's it, unless there's a death."

The COVID-19 vaccines, however aren't on the list of eligible vaccines.

Reiss said the best fix would be to change the VICP's rulebook to add COVID vaccines to its list of covered inoculations. "That will require legislative change. "I hope that legislative change happens."

Chapter 2

I would like to begin this book starting with *Professor Michel Chossudovsky's* take on the COVID Pandemic. He is an award-winning author, Professor of Economics, and Founder of the Centre For Research on Globalization.

This is what he says in part about the COVID-19 crisis. An excerpt from one of his video talks speaks as follows:

We are at the crossroads of one of the most serious crises in history. The incitement of untrue events has erupted worldwide. People have been misled by government and media that the COVID-19 virus is the reason for this lockdown crisis. There is a new world order that is taking over. Closing down the economy, schools, small, and medium size businesses, and all performing arts as a means of combating the virus; that is what they want us to believe. The public is continually being informed that COVID is a "world-wide killer." Yet in most cases the effects are shortness of breath, fever, and mild illness. Only a small percentage of the American population has become critically ill. All 190 countries taking part in this global deceit are members of the UN, inciting lie after lie that we are in a world crisis. There is absolutely no scientific basis for this. Yet these ridiculously low numbers are used to spearhead a worldwide panic. International financial institutions play a key role in this. This crisis triggered the halting of air travel, trade relations, shipping, and manufacturing. When the pandemic first began in January of 2020, COVID cases were very low. When the World Health

PANDEMIC PANDEMONIUM

Organization declared a worldwide epidemic, there were only about 44,000 cases out of a population of 6.4 billion reported. Small enterprises were driven into bankruptcy and people began going into massive unemployment. Fear campaigns went into high gear. The collapse of a world economy became devastating. The health impact of this system is also devastating and far surpasses the scant estimates of COVID yet we are told that the numbers are far, far greater than they actually are. One might reasonably argue there is a national health crisis that is part of a global problem which requires coordinated government intervention but the actual statistics that reveal the low levels of infection and death in most states would not support that contention. How can closing down the entire economy of the U.S. justify this kind of a lockdown? The disruption of trade, infrastructure, social services, and the destabilization of the economy is the justification combating the virus. Those lies were substantiated by a massive media campaign called "social engineering." And the numbers were hiked up to justify a second wave.

As we face the most devastating crisis in history, free speech is suppressed by online censorship. Medical doctors who object are categorized as social psychopaths. If you express reservations regarding social distancing, face masks, and are against inoculation, we open ourselves up for attack by our friends, neighbors and families who have been brainwashed by the media. Censorship indulges those beliefs because we are shut off from the voices of doctors, scientists, and professors who are of a different opinion. People on social media who question anything, are taken down. The practice of taking down YouTube videos has become widespread. This constitutes censorship. Twitter has confirmed that it will remove all posts that suggest that there are adverse impacts to the vaccinations. This diabolical warfare has led us into a spiraling debt and big money corporations are the driving forces. Using today's technologies undermines democracy without the need for military intervention. Super billionaires are getting the assets of bankrupt companies and this is their agenda. Although there is absolutely no scientific reason for closing down entire countries, it persists. The media and governments are lying. It is time for everyone to come out of this collective hysteria which are killing many more people than COVID. Why are we sometimes told we don't need to wear masks? What changes? Science doesn't change, politics changes. Governments lie and once the lie becomes the truth there is no going back. The world is turned upside down, and insanity prevails. The fear campaign prevails and people are now led to believe that normalcy will be restored once the entire population has been vaccinated. Were there standard animal lab tests conducted or did the vaccine go straight to human guinea pigs? Only a few months is unheard of for testing a new vaccine.

Chapter 3

Dr. Joseph Mercola is an American alternative medicine proponent. He received his medical degree from Chicago College of Osteopathic Medicine and has been in practice for over thirty-five years. He specializes in educating the public about how to apply natural solutions and avoid the dangers of pharmaceutical medicine. However, Dr. Mercola has also received bad press as he has become a vehement and vociferous speaker against the COVID-19 pandemic. In fact, one such quotation read as follows: "Dr. Mercola: An anti-vaccine quack tycoon pivots effortlessly to profit by spreading COVID-19 misinformation."

However, I have chosen to post some of his views in this chapter, simply because I am familiar with some of his health regimens which I myself have used. As a result, I became a fan of his through the years. Despite the "expert" opinions which oppose him, Dr. Mercola has authored many books on the subject of health and immunity, including three N.Y. Times Best sellers.

Dr. Mercola:

"Vaccine makers have nothing to lose by marketing their experimental COVID-19 shots as they have full indemnity for injuries occurring from the vaccines under the Public Readiness and Emergency Preparedness Act (PREP) passed in the U.S. in 2005.

Countries that purchase COVID-19 vaccinations must sign agreements with Pfizer that are confidential. Pfizer's efforts to develop and manufacture the product could have significant risks and uncertainties. In the event that another drug or treatment comes out that can prevent or cure COVID-19, the agreement states, the country must follow through with their order. Ivermectin for instance, is not only safe, inexpensive, widely available, and has been found to reduce COVID mortality by 81%. It continues to be ignored in favor of the more expensive, yet less effective treatments of this experimental vaccine. Even if Pfizer fails to deliver vaccine doses within their estimated delivery time, the purchaser (country) may not cancel the order. The purchaser of COVID-19 must acknowledge two facts. That both their efficacy and risks are unknown and that the long-term effects are also currently not known. It is also widely known that you cannot sue Pfizer if you have severe COVID vaccine side effects. Because the contracts are so ironclad, Pfizer cannot be held responsible, and in fact is immune from any lawsuits pertaining to vaccine side effects or deaths. One question we should be asking is this: If the COVID-19 vaccines are as safe and effective as manufacturers claim, why do they require this level of indemnification?"

Dr. Mercola also points out:

"Natural immunity offers robust protection against all variants, whereas vaccine-induced immunity can't. The reason for this is because when you recover from the natural infection, you have both antibodies and T cells against all parts of the virus, not just the spike protein."

"If we are to depend on vaccine-induced immunity, as public health officials are urging us to do, we'll end up in a never-ending booster treadmill."

"It makes no sense to require vaccinations for the previously infected."

"My goal is to empower you to take control of your health by providing trustworthy natural health information and advocating for *your right* to making informed health choices."

Chapter 4

As a world-renowned lawyer, *Dr. Reiner Fuellmich* has been admitted to the Bar in Germany and in California for 26 years and has practiced law primarily as a trial lawyer against fraudulent corporations. One is Deutsche Bank, formerly one of the world's largest and most respected banks, and today one of the most toxic criminal organizations in the world. Another is VW, one of the world's largest and most respected car manufacturers in the world, today notorious for its giant diesel fraud, and Kuehne & Nagel, the world's largest shipping company, in a multi-million-dollar bribery case.

"I am one of four members of the German Corona Investigative Committee. Since July 10, 2020, this committee has been listening to a large number of international scientists' and experts' testimony to find answers to questions about the corona crisis, which more and more people worldwide are asking. All of the above-named cases of corruption and fraud committed by German corporations pale in comparison in view of the extent of the damage the corona crisis has caused and continues to cause.

This corona crisis, according to all we know today, must be renamed a "Corona Scandal" and those responsible for it must be prosecuted and sued for civil damages. On a political level, everything must be done to make sure that no one will ever again be in a position of such power as to be able to defraud humanity or to attempt to manipulate us with their corrupt agendas. And for this reason, I will now explain to you how and where the international network of lawyers will argue this biggest tort case ever, the corona fraud scandal, which has meanwhile unfolded into probably the greatest crime against humanity ever committed.

Crimes against humanity are today regulated in section 7 of the International Criminal Code. The three major questions to be answered in the contest of a judicial approach to the corona scandal are:

1. Is there a corona pandemic or is there only a PCR test pandemic? Specifically does a positive PCR test result mean that the person tested is infected with COVID-19, or does it mean absolutely nothing in connection with the COVID-19 infection?

2. Do the so-called anti-corona measures, such as the lockdown, mandatory face masks, social distancing, and quarantine regulations, serve to protect the world's population from corona, or do these measures serve only to make people panic so they believe—without asking any questions—that their lives are in danger, so in the end the pharmaceutical and tech industries can generate huge profits from the sale of PCR tests, antigen and antibody tests and vaccines, as well as the harvesting of our genetic fingerprints?

3. Is it true that the German government has massively lobbied, more than any other country, by the chief protagonists of this so-called corona pandemic because Germany is known as a particularly disciplined country and was therefore to become a role model for the rest of the world for its strict and successful adherence to the corona measures?

Answers to these three questions are urgently needed because the allegedly new and highly dangerous corona virus has not caused any excess mortality anywhere in the world, and certainly not in Germany. But the anti-corona measures, whose only basis are the PCR test results which are in turn all based on the German Drosten test, have destroyed the economic existence of countless companies and individuals worldwide. In Australia for example, people are thrown into prison if they do not wear a mask or do not wear it properly as deemed by the authorities. In the Philippines, people who do not wear a mask or who do not wear it properly, in this sense, are getting shot in the head.

Let me first give you a summary of the facts as they present themselves today. The most important thing in a lawsuit is to establish the facts—that is to find out what actually happened. That is because the application of the law always depends on the facts at issue. If I want to prosecute someone for fraud, I cannot do that by presenting the facts of a car accident. So, what happened here regarding the alleged corona pandemic?

The facts laid out below are, to a large extent, the result of the work of the Corona Investigative Committee was founded on July 10, 2020 by four lawyers in order to determine, through hearing expert testimony of international scientists and other experts:

1. How dangerous is the virus really?
2. What is the significance of a PCR test?
3. What collateral damage has been caused by the corona measures, both with respect to the world population's health, and with respect to the world's economy?

Let me start with a little bit of background information. What happened in May 2019 and then in early 2020? And what happened 12 years earlier with the swine flu which many of you may have forgotten about? In May 2019 the stronger of the two parties which govern Germany in a grand coalition, the CDU, held a Congress on Global Health, apparently at the instigation of important players from the pharmaceutical industry and from the tech industry. At this Congress, the usual suspects, you might say, gave their speeches. The German Secretary of Health was there. But, some other people, whom one would not necessarily expect to be present at such a gathering, were also there: A leading virologist from the Charite hospital in Berlin; a veterinarian and Head of the RKI (the German equivalent of the CDC) as well as a well-known person from the World Health Organization (WHO). They all gave speeches there. Also present and giving speeches were the chief lobbyists of the world's two largest health funds, namely the Bill and Melinda Gates Foundation and the Welcome Trust. Less than a year later these very people called the shots in the proclamation of the worldwide corona pandemic and made sure that mass PCR tests were used to prove mass infections with COVID-19 all over the world, and are now pushing for vaccines to be invented and sold worldwide.

These infections, or rather positive test results that the PCR tests delivered, in turn became the justification for worldwide lockdowns, social distancing and mandatory face masks. It is important to note at this point that the definition of a pandemic was changed 12 years earlier. Until then, a pandemic was considered to be a disease that spread worldwide and which led to many serious illnesses and deaths. Suddenly, and for reasons never explained, it was supposed to be a worldwide disease only.

Many serious illnesses and many deaths were not required any more to announce a pandemic. Due to this change, the WHO, which is closely intertwined with the global pharmaceutical industry, was able to declare the swine flu pandemic in 2009, with the result that vaccines were produced and sold worldwide on the basis of contracts that have been kept secret until today.

These vaccines proved to be completely unnecessary because the swine flu eventually turned out to be a mild flu, and never became the horrific plague that the pharmaceutical industry and its affiliated universities kept announcing it would turn into, with millions of deaths certain to happen if people didn't get vaccinated. These vaccines also led to serious health problems. About 700 children in Europe fell incurably ill with narcolepsy and are now forever severely disabled. The vaccines bought with millions of taxpayers' money had to be destroyed with even more taxpayers' money. Already then, during the swine flu the German virologist Drosten was one of those who stirred up panic in the population, repeating over and over again that the swine flu would claim many hundreds of thousands, even millions of deaths all over the world. In the end, it was mainly thanks to a member of the German Bundestag, and also a member of the Council of Europe, that this was brought to an end before it would lead to even more serious consequences.

Fast forward to March 2020, when the German Bundestag announced an Epidemic Situation of National Importance, which is the German equivalent of a pandemic in March of 2020 and, based on this, the lockdown with the suspension of all essential constitutional rights for an unforeseeable time, there was only one single opinion on which the Federal Germany based its decision. In an outrageous violation of the universally accepted principle "audiatur et altera pars," which means that one must also hear the other side, the only person they listened to was the German virologist.

That is the very person whose prognoses had proved to be completely false 12 years earlier. We know this because a whistleblower and a member of the Green Party, told us about it. He did so first on August 2, 2020 in Berlin, in the context of an event at which Robert F. Kennedy, Jr. also took part, and at which both men gave speeches. And he did so afterwards in one of the sessions of the Corona Committee.

The reason he did this is that he had become increasingly skeptical about the official narrative propagated by politicians and the mainstream media. He had therefore undertaken an effort to find out about other scientists' opinions and had found them on the Internet. There he realized that there were a number of highly renowned scientists who had a completely different opinion, which contradicted his prognoses. They assumed—and still do assume—that there was no disease that went beyond the gravity of the seasonal flu, that the population had already acquired cross—or—T—cell immunity against this allegedly new virus, and that there was therefore no reason for any special measures, and certainly not for vaccinations.

These scientists include Professor John Ioannidis of Stanford University in California, a specialist in statistics and epidemiology, as well as public health, and at the same time the most quoted scientist in the world; Professor Michael Levitt, a Nobel-prize winner for chemistry and also a biophysicist at Sanford University; the German professors Kary Molling, Sucharit Bhakti, Klud Wittkowski, as well as Stefan Homburg; and now many, many more scientists and doctors worldwide, including Dr. Mike Yeadon. Dr. Mike Yeadon is the former Vice-President and Scientific Director of Pfizer, one of the largest pharmaceutical companies in the world. (I will reveal more about Dr. Yeadon in a later chapter).

At the end of March, beginning of April 2020, a certain doctor turned to the leadership of the Green Party with the knowledge he had accumulated, and suggested that they present these other scientific opinions to the public and explain that, contrary to the virologist's doomsday prophecies, there was no reason for the public to panic. Incidentally, Lord Sumption, who served as a judge at the British Supreme Court from 2012 to 2018, had done the very same thing at the very same time and had come to the very same conclusion: That there was no factual basis for panic and no legal basis for the corona measures.

Now let's take a look at the current actual situation regarding the virus's danger, the complete uselessness of PCR tests for the detection of infections, and the lockdowns based on non-existent infections. In the meantime, we know that the health care systems were never in danger of becoming overwhelmed by COVID-19. On the contrary, many hospitals remain empty to this day and some are now facing bankruptcy. The hospital ship Comfort, which anchored in New York at the time, and could have accommodated a thousand patients, never accommodated more than some 20 patients. Nowhere was there any excess mortality. Studies carried out by Professor Ioannidis and others have shown that the mortality or corona is equivalent to that of the seasonal flu. Even the pictures from Bergamo and New York that were used to demonstrate to the world that panic was in order proved to be deliberately misleading.

Then, the so-called "Panic Paper" was leaked, which was written by the German Department of the Interior. Its classic content shows beyond a shadow of a doubt that, in fact, the population was deliberately driven to panic by politicians and mainstream media. The accompanying irresponsible statements by the head of the RKI (Robert Koch Institute) who repeatedly and excitedly announced that the corona measures must be followed unconditionally by the population without them asking any questions. In his public statements, he kept announcing that the situation was very grave and threatening, although the figures compiled by his own Institute said the exact opposite. The Robert Koch Institute is the governments central scientific institute in the field of biomedicine. It is one of the most important bodies for the safeguarding of public health in Germany.

In Bergamo, the vast majority of deaths, 94% to be exact, turned out to be the result not of COVID-19, but rather consequence of the government deciding to transfer sick patients, sick with probably the cold or seasonal flu, from hospitals to nursing homes in order to make room at the hospitals for all the COVID patients who ultimately never arrived. In addition, a flu vaccination, which had previously been administered, had further weakened the immune systems of the people in the nursing homes. In New York, only some, but by far not all the hospitals were overwhelmed. Many people, most of whom were again elderly, and had serious pre-existing medical conditions, and most of whom, had it not been for the panic-mongering, would have just stayed at home to recover, raced to the hospitals. There, many of them fell victim to healthcare-associated infections or nosocomial infections on the one hand, and incidents of mal-practice on the other hand, for example, by being put on a respirator rather than receiving oxygen through an oxygen mask.

Again, to clarify: COVID-19, in this current state of affairs, is a dangerous disease, just like the seasonal flu is a dangerous disease. And of course, COVID-19, just like the seasonal flu, may sometimes take a severe clinical course and will sometimes kill patients. However, as autopsies have shown, which were carried out in Germany in particular, by a forensic scientist in Hamburg, the fatalities he examined had almost all been caused by serious pre-existing conditions, and almost all of the people who had died had died at a very old age, just like in Italy, meaning they had lived beyond their average life expectancy.

In this context, the following should also be mentioned: The German RKI—that is, again the equivalent of the CDC—had initially, strangely enough, recommended that no autopsies be performed. And there are numerous credible reports that doctors and hospitals worldwide have been paid money for declaring a diseased person a victim of COVID-19 rather than write down the true cause of death on the death certificate, for example a heart attack or a gunshot wound. Without the autopsies, we would never know that the overwhelming majority of the alleged COVID-19 victims had died of completely different diseases, but not of COVID-19. The assertion that the lockdown was necessary because there were so many different infections with SARS-COV-2, and because the healthcare systems would be overwhelmed is wrong for three reasons, as we have learned from the hearings we conducted with the Corona Committee, and from other data that has become available in the meantime.

A. A lockdown was imposed when the virus was already retreating. By the time the lockdown was imposed, the alleged infection rates were already dropping again.

B. There's already protection from the virus because of cross—or T—cell immunity in the general population against the corona viruses contained in every flu or influenza wave. This is true, even if this time around, a slightly different strain of the coronavirus was at work. And that is because the body's own immune system remembers every virus it has ever battled in the past, and from this experience, it also recognizes a supposedly new, but still similar, strain of the virus from the corona family. Incidentally, that's how the PCR test for the detection of an infection was invented by Professor Drosten.

At the beginning of January 2020, based on this very basic knowledge, a PCR test was developed which supposedly detects an infection with SARS-COV-2 without ever having seen the real Wuhan virus from China, only having learned from social media reports that there was something going on in Wuhan. The German virologist whom we previously spoke about started tinkering on his computer with what would become "his" corona PCR test. For this he used an old SARS virus, hoping it would be sufficiently similar to the allegedly new strain of the coronavirus found in Wuhan. Then he sent the result of his computer tinkering to China to determine whether the victims of the alleged coronavirus tested positive. They did.

And that was enough for the World Health Organization to sound the pandemic alarm and to recommend the worldwide use of the PCR test for the detection of infections with the new virus now called SARS-COV-2. Drosten's opinion and advice was—this must be emphasized once again. Germany apparently became the center of especially massive lobbying by the pharmaceutical and tech industry because the world, with reference to the allegedly disciplined Germans, should do as the Germans do in order to survive the pandemic.

C. And this is the most important part of our fact-finding: the PCR test is being used on the basis for false statements, NOT based on specific facts with respect to infections. In the meantime, we have learned that these PCR tests do not give any indication of an infection with any virus, let alone an infection with SARS-COV-2. Not only are PCR tests expressly not approved for diagnostic purposes, as is correctly noted on leaflets coming with these tests, and as the inventor of the PCR test, Kary Mullus had repeatedly emphasized. Instead, they're simply incapable of diagnosing any disease; that a positive PCR test result does not mean that they are infected with anything, let alone the contagious SARS-COV-2 virus. Even the United States CDC agrees with this, and I quote directly from one of its publications on the corona virus and the PCR tests, dated

July 13, 2020. First bulletin point says:

Detection of Viral mRNA may not indicate the presence of infectious virus or that 2019 nCOV (novel coronavirus) is the causative agent for clinical symptoms.

Second bulletin point says:

The performance of this test has not been established for monitoring treatment of 2019 nCOV infection. Third point bulletin says: "This test cannot rule out diseases caused by other bacterial or viral pathogens."

It is still not clear whether there has ever been a scientifically correct isolation of the Wuhan virus, so that nobody knows exactly what we're looking for when we test, especially since this virus, just like the flu viruses, mutates quickly. The PCR swabs take one or two sequences of a molecule that are invisible to the human eye and therefore need to be amplified in many cycles to make it visible.

Everything over 35 cycles is—as reported by the New York Times and others—considered completely unreliable and scientifically unjustifiable. However, the PCR test, as well as the WHO recommended tests that followed his example, are set to 45 cycles. Can that be because of the desire to produce as many positive results as possible and therefore provide the basis for the false assumption that a large number of infections have been detected?

The test cannot distinguish inactive and reproductive matter. That means that a positive result may happen because the test detects, for example, a piece of debris, a fragment of the molecule, which may signal nothing else than that the immune system of the person tested won a battle with a common cold in the past.

In an interview with a German business magazine in 2014, at that time concerning the alleged detection of an infection with a MERS virus and allegedly with the help of the PCR test, that these PCR tests are so highly sensitive that even very healthy and non-infectious people may test positive.

In short, this test cannot detect any information, contrary to all false claims stating that it can. An infection, a so-called "hot" infection, requires that the virus, or rather a fragment of a molecule which may be a virus, is not just found somewhere, for example, in the throat of a person without causing any damage—that would be a "cold" infection. Rather, a "hot" infection requires that the virus penetrates into the cells, replicates there and causes symptoms such as headaches or sore throat. Only then is a person really infected in the sense of a "hot" infection, because only then is a person contagious, that is, able to infect others. Until then, it is completely harmless for both the host and all other people that the host comes into contact with. Once again, this means that positive test results, contrary to all other claims, mean nothing with respect to infections, as even the CDC knows, as quoted above.

Meanwhile, a number of highly respected scientists worldwide assume that there has never been a corona pandemic, but only a PCR test pandemic. This is the conclusion reached by many German scientists, such as professors Bhakti, Reiss,

Molling, Hockertz, Walach and many others, including the above-mentioned John Ioannidis, and the Nobel laureate, Professor Michael Levitt from Stanford University.

The most recent such opinion is that of the aforementioned Dr. Mike Yeadon, who worked as a scientific researcher and Vice-President at Pfizer, who held this position for 16 years. He and his co-authors all well-known scientists published a scientific paper of September of 2020 and he wrote a corresponding magazine article on September 20, 2020. Among other things, he and they state—and I quote: "We're basing our government policy, our economic policy, and the policy of restricting fundamental rights, presumably on completely wrong data and assumptions about the coronavirus. If it weren't for the test results that are constantly reported in the media, the pandemic would be over because nothing really happened. Of course, there are some serious individual cases of illness, but there are also some in every flu epidemic.

There was a real wave of disease in March and April, but since then, everything has gone back to normal. Only the positive results rise and sink wildly, again and again, depending on how many tests are carried out. But the real cases of illnesses are over. There can be no talk of a second wave. The allegedly new strain of the coronavirus is..."—Dr. Yeadon continues—"...only new in that it is a new type of the long-known coronavirus.

There are at least four coronaviruses that are epidemic and cause some of the common colds we experience, especially in winter. They all have a striking sequence similarly to the virus that has now allegedly been newly discovered, a T-cell immunity has long existed in this respect. 30 per cent of the population had this before the allegedly new virus ever appeared. Therefore, it is sufficient for the so-called herd immunity that 15 to 25 percent of the population are infected with the allegedly new coronavirus to stop the further spread of the virus. And this has long been the case: *The Deadly Danger of False Positives.*

September 20, 2020, and I quote him: "The likelihood of an apparently positive case being a false positive is between 89 to 94% per cent near certainty."

Dr. Yeadon, in agreement with the professors of immunology; Kamera from Germany, Kappel from the Netherlands, and Cahill from Ireland, as well as the microbiologist Dr. Arve from Australia, all of whom testified before the German Corona Committee, explicitly points out that a positive test does not mean that an intact virus has been found. The authors explain that what the PCR test actually measures is — and I quote: 'Simply the presence of partial RNA sequences present in the intact virus, which cannot make the subject sick, and cannot be transmitted, and cannot make anyone else sick.'

Because of the complete unsuitability of the test for the detection of infectious diseases, Oxford Professor Carl Heneghan, Director of the Centre for Evidence Based Medicine, writes that the COVID virus would never disappear if this test practice were to be continued, but would always be falsely detected in much of what is tested. Lockdowns, as Yeadon and his colleagues found out, do not work. Sweden with its laissez-faire approach, and Great Britain, with its strict lockdown, for example, have completely comparable disease and mortality statistics. The same was found by U.S. scientists concerning the different U.S. states. It makes no difference to the incidence of disease whether a state implements a lockdown or not.

If the PCR tests had not been used as a diagnostic tool for corona infections, there would not be a pandemic and there would be no lockdowns, but everything would have been perceived as a medium or light wave of influenza which scientists conclude. Dr. Yeadon, in his piece *The Deadly Danger Of False Positives*, writes: This test is fatally flawed and must immediately be withdrawn and never used again in this setting, unless shown to be fixed. And, towards the end of that article, "I have explained how a hopelessly performing diagnostic test has been, and continues to be used, not for diagnosis of disease, but it seems solely to create fear."

Now let's take a look at the current actual situation regarding the severe damage caused by the lockdowns and other measures. Another detailed paper, written by a German official in the Department of the Interior, who is responsible for risk assessment and the protection of the population against risks, was leaked recently. It is now called the "False Alarm" paper. This paper comes to the conclusion that there was, and is, no sufficient evidence for serious health risks for the population but, the author says, there's very much evidence of the corona measures causing gigantic health and economic damage to the population, which he then describes in detail in this paper. This, he concludes, will lead to very high claims for damages, which the government will be responsible for. This has now become reality, but the paper's author was suspended.

More and more scientists, but also lawyers, recognize that, as a result of the deliberate panic-mongering, and the corona measures enabled by this panic, democracy is in great danger of being replaced by fascist totalitarian models. As I already mentioned above, in Australia, people who do not wear masks, which more and more studies show, are hazardous to health, or who allegedly do not wear them correctly, are handcuffed and thrown into jail. In the Philippines, they run the risk of getting shot, but even in Germany and in other previously civilized countries, children are taken away from their parents if they do not comply with quarantine regulations, distance regulations, and mask-wearing regulations. According to the psychologists and psychotherapists who testified before the Corona Committee, children are traumatized en masse, with the worst psychological consequences yet to be expected in the medium—long-term. In Germany alone, bankruptcies are expected in the fall, to strike small-medium-sized businesses, which form the backbone of the economy. This will result in incalculable taxes losses and incalculably high-and long-term social security money transfers for—among other things—unemployment benefits.

Let me now give you a summary of the legal consequences. The most difficult part of a lawyer's work is always to establish true facts, not the application of the legal rules to these facts. Unfortunately, a German lawyer does not learn this at law school but the Anglo-Americans do get the necessary training for this at their law schools. And probably, for this reason, but also because of the much more pronounced independence of the Anglo-American judiciary, the Anglo-American law of evidence is much more effective in practice than the German one.

A court of law can only decide a legal dispute correctly if it has previously determined the facts correctly, which is not possible without looking at all the evidence. And that's why the law of evidence is so important. On the basis of the facts summarized above, in particular those established with the help of the work of the German Corona Committee, the legal evaluation is actually simple. It is simple for all civilized legal systems, regardless of whether these legal systems are based on civil law, which follows the Roman law more closely, or whether they are based on Anglo-American common law, which is loosely connected to the Roman law.

Let's take a look at the unconstitutionality of the measures. A number of German professors have stated, either in written expert opinions or in interviews, that these measures—the corona measures—are without a sufficient factual basis, and also without a sufficient legal basis and therefore unconstitutional and must be repealed immediately. Very recently, a prominent judge declared publicly that the German judiciary, just like the general public, has also been so panic-stricken that it was no longer able to administer justice properly. He says that the courts of law—and I quote—"have all too quickly waived through coercive measures which, for millions of people, all over Germany, represent massive suspensions of their constitutional rights." He points out that

German citizens—again I quote—"are currently experiencing the most serious encroachment of their constitutional rights since the founding of the federal republic of Germany in 1949." In order to contain the corona pandemic, federal and state governments have intervened massively, and in part, threatening the very existence of the country as it is guaranteed by the constitutional rights of the people.

What about fraud, intentional infliction of damage and crimes against humanity? Based on the rules of criminal law, asserting false facts concerning the PCR tests or international misrepresentation can only be assessed as fraud. Based on the rules of civil tort law, this translates into intentional infliction of damage. A prominent German professor of civil law supports this finding in public interviews. In a comprehensive legal opinion of around 180 pages, he has familiarized himself with the subject matter like no other legal scholar has done thus far and, in particular, has provided a detailed account of the complete failure of the mainstream media to report on the true facts of this so-called pandemic.

Although the PCR tests cannot provide any information about infections, but asserted over and over again to the general public that they can, with their counterparts all over the world repeating this. And they all knew and accepted that, on the basis of their recommendations, the governments of the world would decide on lockdowns, the rules for social distancing, and mandatory wearing of masks, the latter representing a very serious health hazard, as more and more independent studies and expert statements show. Under the rules off civil tort law, all those who have been harmed by these PCR-test-induced lockdowns are entitled to receive full compensation for their losses. In particular, there is a duty to compensate—that is, a duty to pay damages for the loss of profits suffered by companies and self-employed persons as a result of the lockdown and other measures.

In the meantime, however, the anti-corona measures have caused, and continue to cause, such devasting damage to the world's population's health and economy that the crimes committed by the WHO must be legally qualified as actual crimes against humanity, as defined in section 7 of the International Criminal Code.

How can we do something? What can we do? Well, the class action is the best route to compensatory damages and to political consequences. The so-called class action lawsuit is based on English law and exists today in the USA and in Canada. It enables a court of law to allow a complaint for damages to be tried as a class action lawsuit at the request of a plaintiff if:

1. As a result of a damage-inducing event . . .

2. A large number of people suffer the same damage.

Phrased differently, a judge can allow a class-action lawsuit to go forward if common questions of law and fact make up the vital component of the lawsuit. Here, the common questions of law and fact revolve around the worldwide PCR-test-based lockdowns and its consequences. Just like the VW diesel passenger cars were functioning products, but they were defective due to a so-called defeat device because they didn't comply with emission standards, so too the PCR tests—which are perfectly good products in other settings—are defective products when it comes to the diagnosis of infections. Now, if an American or Canadian company or an American or Canadian individual decides to sue these persons in the United States or Canada for damages, then the court called upon to resolve this dispute may, upon request, allow this complaint to be tried as a class action lawsuit. If this happens, all affected parties worldwide will be informed about this through publications in the mainstream media and will thus have the opportunity to join this class action within a certain period of time, to be determined by the court. It should be emphasized that nobody MUST join the class action, but every injured party CAN join the class action.

The advantage of the class action is that only one trial is needed, namely to try the complaint of a representative plaintiff who is affected in a manner typical of everyone else in the class. This is, firstly, cheaper, and secondly, faster than hundreds of thousands or more individual lawsuits. And thirdly, it imposes less of a burden on the courts. Fourthly, as a rule it allows a much more precise examination of the accusations than would be possible in the context of hundreds of thousands, or more likely in this corona setting, even millions of individual lawsuits.

In particular, the well-established and proven Anglo-American law of evidence, with its pre-trial discovery, is applicable. This requires that all evidence relevant for the determination of the lawsuit is put on the table. In contrast to the typical situation in German lawsuits with structural imbalance, that is, lawsuits involving on the one hand a consumer, and on the other hand a powerful corporation, the withholding or even destruction of evidence is not without consequence; rather the party withholding or even destroying evidence loses the case under these evidence rules.

Here in Germany, a group of tort lawyers have banded together to help their clients with recovery damages. They have provided all relevant information and forms for German plaintiffs to both estimate how much damage they have suffered and join the group or class of plaintiffs who will later join the class when it goes forward either in Canada or the U.S. Initially, this group of lawyers had considered to also collect and manage the claims for damages, of other non-German plaintiffs, but this proved to be unmanageable.

However, through an international lawyers' network, which is growing larger by the day, the German group of attorneys provides to all of their colleagues in all other countries, free of charge, all relevant information, including expert opinions and testimonies of experts showing that the PCR tests cannot detect infections. And they also provide them with all relevant information as to how they can prepare and bundle the claims for damages of their clients, so that, they too, can assert their clients' claims for damages, either in their home country's courts of law or within the framework of the class-action, as explained above.

These scandalous corona facts, gathered mostly by the Corona Committee and summarized above, are the very same facts that will soon be proven to be true either in one court of law, or in many courts of law all over the world.

These are the facts that will pull the masks off the faces of all those responsible for these crimes. To the politicians who believe these corrupt people, these facts are hereby offered as a lifeline that can help you readjust your course of action, and start the long overdue public scientific discussion, and not go down with those charlatans and criminals."

I viewed Dr. Fuellmich on a huge video screen as he spoke to a crowd in Trafalgar Square to thousands of people. He specified that class action lawsuits are underway in the U.S. and Canada. He also stated that institutions and individuals, especially those responsible for the PCR tests, particularly in Europe and the U.S. are the basis for governments lying and the manipulating of the up-and-down "infection" figures leading to false numbers about hospitalizations and deaths about a virus which is less dangerous than the common flu.

Mr. Fuellmich closed his talk on a positive and encouraging note. "It is humanity versus inhumanity. We are all human. We laugh, we cry, we sing, and hug. The other side can't. The other side has no access to the spiritual side. Therefore, the other side, without any doubt, the inhuman side, will lose this inhuman battle for life."

Chapter 5

Dr. Russel Blaylock is a nationally recognized board-certified neurosurgeon, health practitioner, author, and lecturer who writes as follows:

There are four major companies offering the COVID-19 vaccines; Pfizer, Moderna, Johnson & Johnson and AstraZeneca. Both Pfizer and Moderna use a technology never before approved called a messenger RNA (mRNA) biological. The mRNA biologicals encase spike protein producing mRNA with a spike producing nanoparticle capsule—LNP which contains nano-sized polyethylene glycol to protect the mRNA from enzymatic destruction by the vaccinated person's cells. This prolongs the survival of the mRNA, allowing it to continually produce the spike protein in your body. The latter two biologicals from Johnson & Johnson and AstraZeneca utilize a single vaccine technology involving the use of an altered attenuated virus (Adeno26) to generate antibodies to the spike protein.

This man-made virus literally infects the person with a spike protein containing virus. You should know that the spike protein is the pathological part of the COVID-19 virus. In essence, you have a man-made virus and mRNA biological that does exactly what the COVID-19 virus does to you. It exposes you to massive amounts of spike protein. Once in the body this spike protein can enter all tissues, including the heart, the brain, the lungs, the kidneys, the eyes, and the liver. The two main sites it invades with the spike protein are the liver and the spleen—both are major immune regulating sites. No studies have been done on what happens to the spike proteins once they have been injected and most important, how long the mRNA will continue producing spike proteins. Moderna and Johnson & Johnson have never made a vaccine before this. Most important, one should understand these are experimental vaccines.

In order to allow the population to use these entirely experimental biologicals, the government had to declare this "pandemic" a medical emergency. The vaccine approval process for an experimental vaccine normally requires a period for as long as ten years of intensive study before a vaccine is approved. As mentioned, the pharmaceutical companies did not conduct studies to see how the injected biologicals were distributed in the body or how long the immune stimulation would continue which is absolutely vital with regard to safety and the risk of long terms side effects.

Vaccine manufacture has become the major profit maker for pharmaceutical companies especially for vaccines that are recommended or mandated each year. This has already been proposed for this set of vaccines. This is especially so now that these companies have been given legal protection from lawsuits by Congress. Of most importance is that this virus is being treated as if it were a deadly pandemic of major proportions. Unfortunately, most people do not understand the concept of a "pandemic." Most people assume that any virus that spreads rapidly over the entire globe qualifies. If this were so, the common cold viruses would constitute a pandemic several times a year.

Chapter 6

While unemployment is rising and strains on household budgets have perhaps eased in recent months, the employment rate still remains low and millions still report that their households did not get enough to eat or they are not caught up on rent payments.

AAP News and Journals Gateway reported as follows:

Melissa Jenco, News Content Editor

Study - COVID-19 pandemic exacerbated hardships for low-income, minority families.

Financial hardships caused by the COVID-19 pandemic were hitting low income, black and Hispanic families especially hard, according to a new report. Job losses have left families struggling to pay for necessities like housing, food, and medical care. The findings come from a nationally representative Urban Institute survey of just over 9,000 adults in March and April, which was released in a new report. "The COVID-19 crisis has caused significant disruption to children's daily lives, and the findings in this brief underscore the many ways in which the pandemic poses risk to children's health, well-being and development."

Roughly 43% of parents living with children reported they or a family member has lost a job or work hours due to the pandemic. That includes 62% of Hispanic families, 50% of black families and 36.5% of white families. Just over half of low-income families and one-third of higher income families reported job losses. While 41.5% of those who are employed can work from home, only about one- quarter of low-income and Hispanic parents could do so. Roughly 65% of all families had paid sick leave, but only half of low-income and Hispanic families had this benefit.

About one-third of all families said someone in the household stayed home from work to watch the children because of the outbreak while 16.5% had trouble arranging childcare. Again, low-income and Hispanic families were most likely to report difficulty arranging care. Surveys also found about one-third of families experienced a material hardship in the past month, a rate that rises to about half of low-income, black and Hispanic families.

One quarter of families experienced food insecurity, including more than one-third of low-income, black and Hispanic families. Roughly 10.5% of all families were late with their rent or mortgage payment and didn't pay the full amount, 13% didn't pay the full amount of their utility bills and 16% had someone go without medical care due to the cost.

Authors said the pandemic exacerbated material hardship and psychological distress for low-income families, and warned such stress can have long-lasting impact on children. They called for increased Supplemental Nutrition Assistance Program benefits, school meal-service during the summer, Medicaid expansion, mortgage/rent assistance, expanded federal paid leave policies and child care programs for essential workers. They also said support should not hinge on immigration status.

The authors concluded: "Ensuring children's home environments remain as stable as possible and that their educational, nutritional, physical and mental health needs will be paramount to helping families and communities weather the current crisis, and to minimizing adverse, economic health, and emotional effects on children."

PANDEMIC PANDEMONIUM

◆ ◆ ◆ ◆ ◆ ◆ ◆ ◆ ◆ ◆

The March 11, 2020 lockdown and its devastating and social economic consequences:

Starting on March 11, 2020, 44,279 so-called confirmed RT-PCR positive cases (worldwide out of China) and 1440 COVID deaths were used to justify:

1. Social confinement
2. The lockdown and closure of 190 national economies, crisis of the global economy
3. Extensive corporate bankruptcies in key sectors of economic activity
4. The outright elimination of small and medium sized enterprises
5. The triggering of poverty and mass unemployment
6. Social distancing, the face mask, no social or family gatherings
7. Devastating impacts on mental health
8. An engineered crisis of the national health system
9. The closure of schools, colleges, and universities
10. The closure of museums, concert halls, cultural and sports events
11. Institutional collapse of the disruption of civil society

The stated objective has always been to save lives. Yet the outcome of these policies have literally destroyed people's lives. Millions of people worldwide have been driven into extreme poverty. And then ten months later the COVID-19 vaccine had come to our rescue.

The mRNA vaccine was presented as an everlasting solution, as a means of curbing the epidemic, saving lives, reopening our shattered national economies and restoring a sense of normality in our daily lives. A massive campaign was initiated in support of the vaccine. A promise of a new life. A return to reason and normalcy. All of this turned out to be an illusion, spearheaded by lies and fabrications.

Chapter 7

F. William Engdahl is an independent political economist specializing for more than 30 years in the geopolitical analysis of international political economy, food, security, economics, energy, and international affairs. He is the author of many international best-selling books. He is active as a consulting political risk economist for major European banks and private investors. Mr. Engdahl writes as follows:

The current scare in the U.K. and EU as well as the USA is a so-called Delta variant of the coronavirus. The only problem is that we are not being told by the relevant authorities anything useful about the variant.

The Delta variant back in May was originally called the Indian variant. It was also blamed for up to 90% of new COVID-19 positive tests in the U.K. which also has a significant Indian population. What is not being told is that in just two months the alleged Delta positives in India dropped dramatically by 400,000 in May to 40,000 in July. Symptoms were said to be suspiciously like that of ordinary hay fever, so the WHO quickly renamed it the Delta variant according to the Greek alphabet just to muddy the waters more.

Similar Delta declines came to the U.K. "Experts" claim it was because terrified Indians stayed at home as only 1-3% of the population had been vaccinated. If you get the impression they are just inventing explanations to feed the vaccine narrative, you are not alone.

It gets worse. Virtually no one in the U.K., India, the EU or the USA who has been claimed to have tested positive for Delta has had a specific Delta variant test; as such a direct variant test does not exist. Complex and very costly tests are claimed to exist, but no proof is offered that they are being used to claim such things as 90% of U.K. cases are Delta. Labs around the world simply do the standard, highly inaccurate PCR tests and health authorities declare it is "Delta." There is no simple test for Delta or any other variant. If that were not true, the CDC or WHO or other health institutes should explain in detail those tests. They haven't. Ask relevant health "experts" how they prove presence of a Delta variant virus. They cannot. Testing labs in the USA admit that they do not test for any variants."

Chapter 8

Danish parliament recently decided in Copenhagen that all corona measures should be ended from October 1, 2021. There will no longer be a mask requirement and the test regime will be abolished. The Danes will no longer have to provide evidence of whether they are vaccinated or unvaccinated or whether they have tested positive of negative.

Denmark's SSI infectious diseases agency said it no longer relied on vaccination to achieve herd immunity in the country. Tyra Grove Krause, the SSI's acting academic director, said a new wave of infections were expected after people return to work and school at the end of this summer, but it should not be cause for alarm. "It will be more reminiscent of the flu" Krause said.

Overall, the current vaccination rate is just under 58.4 percent of fully vaccinated people in Denmark. In Germany, this value is only slightly lower at 54.5 percent (as of August, 8) but vaccine advocates have been persistent in their fear-mongering and pressure the unvaccinated.

Dr. Renate Holzeisen is one of the lawyers litigating against the European Commission which advocates the COVID vaccination. She is also a Barrister in the field of International and European law. She has filed an impressive number of cases related to the COVID-19 vaccine. She strongly recommended that all employers refrain from vaccination pressure or compulsory vaccination, because most of them were "obviously not even aware of the far-reaching legal consequences associated with it."

The fact that the so-called COVID-19 vaccines, according to the official approval documents of the EMA and the European Commission were not developed and approved for the prevention of infection with the SARS-COV-2 virus, but solely to prevent a more severe course of the disease, were conditionally approved for this reason alone, Holzeisen underscored. The official approval documents therefore show that these substances cannot interrupt the chain of infection because the people treated with them can become infected and can thus become infectious. Practice also proves that people who are completely "vaccinated" become infected with the virus and even have the same viral load as those "unvaccinated people" as the CDC (Center for Disease Control and Prevention) among others, has admitted. It is therefore clear that any COVID-19 "compulsory vaccination" actually lacks any justification.

All pressure, including moral pressure (alleged act of solidarity with one's neighbor) is therefore illegal in terms of criminal and liability law based on the official approval documents.

"As a lawyer advising on corporate law, I strongly recommend that every employer stay away from COVID-19 vaccination pressure of compulsory vaccination, because most of them are obviously not even aware of the far-reaching legal consequences associated with it" she said.

Chapter 9

On August 28, 2021, I viewed a video which was sent to me entitled "Dr. Zelenko schools the Israeli Rabbinical Court." In this video he addresses a Court of Orthodox Rabbis:

Dr. Vladamir Zelenko is a board-certified family physician for over twenty years. He has been described by patients as a family doctor to thousands of families. He is also a medical advisor to a volunteer ambulance group in N.Y.C.

Dr. Zalenko addresses the Court:

I have been a family physician to over 6000 patients. I have trained hundreds of physicians who are now training their students, and as a cumulative group we have treated millions of patients successfully. President Trump, Rudy Guiliani, Sean Hannity, and White House Chief of Staff, Mark Meadows, were among my patients. My experience has given me a unique approach to COVID-19 which is keeping people out of the hospital.

Anytime you evaluate anything therapeutic you need to look at it from three perspectives: Is it safe? Does it work? And do you need it? Just because you have the capability, it doesn't mean you have to use it. There has to be a medical necessity. Look at the CDC statistics. Children under 18 that are healthy have a survival rate of 99.98% with no treatment. The influenza virus is more dangerous to children than COVID-19. If you have a demographic that has no risk of dying from an illness, why would you inject them with a death shot?

Two countries in the world that have the most vaccinated citizens are Israel with an 85% rate of vaccination, and the Seychelles, a small Island Nation located in the Indian Ocean, a rate of over 80%. Both countries are experiencing a Delta variant outbreak. So, if you have vaccinated the majority of the population, why are they still having an outbreak? Why would you even give a third shot of the same stuff that didn't work the first two times not even knowing whether or not they work at all?

According to the Salk Institute, when a person receives the injection, the body becomes a spike producing factory, producing trillions of spikes which migrate into the blood vessels; it's basically like little thorns inside your vascular system. As it flows through the blood cells, the cells become damaged. If that happens in the heart you can get a heart attack. If it happens in the brain you can have a stroke. What we're seeing here is that the number one cause of death in the short term is from blood clots. Most of it happens within the first three or four days of the injection. The other problem is that it is causing inflammation in the hearts of young adults. And most disturbing, and according to The New England Journal of Medicine, is the miscarriage rate in the first trimester of pregnant women. The miscarriage rate in the first trimester once they got vaccinated went from 10% to 80%. Understand this: The miscarriage rate of pregnant women in the first trimester when they get vaccinated, goes up by a factor of eight. That is the preliminary data as it is today.

Animal studies that were done with these vaccines show that all the animals responded well in generating antibodies. But when they were challenged however with the virus that they were immunized against, a large percentage of them died. And when that was investigated, it was found that their immune systems had failed. It is called "antibody dependent enhancement." You may argue however, that maybe human beings are different. However, those studies were not done. You are the study. So, if these risks have not been ruled out, why would we vaccinate someone with a potentially destructive lethal substance without ruling out the risks first?

Another component is the long-term consequences. There is definite evidence that it affects fertility. It damages ovarian function and it reduces sperm count. Who knows over time how it will reduce life spans? And just last week a paper came out that said it increases the risk of cancer. Any way you want to look at it, whether it causes blood clots, inflammation of the heart, or miscarriages in the mid-term where it can result in a pathological disastrous immune reaction, or in the long-term, whether it causes cancer, immune diseases or fertility, that's the big concern.

I have received daily death threats. I risked my life, my career, my reputation, and almost my family just to sit here and tell you what I am saying. So, let me summarize: There is no need for this vaccine. As I have stated, children have a 99.98% rate of getting better. Young adults, from the ages of 18 to 45 have a 99.95% of getting better according to the CDC. Someone who has already had COVID and has the antibodies which is a naturally induced immunity, is a billion times more effective than artificially induced immunity through vaccine. So why would I vaccinate someone with a shot that makes inferior antibodies when I already have healthy antibodies? Now, if you look at the high-risk population which has a 7.5% death rate, and treat people within the right time-frame, you reduce the death rate by 85%. So out of 600,000 Americans we could have prevented 510,000 from going to the hospitals.

Chapter 10

While it is understood that viruses mutate, causing variants, French Virologist and Nobel Prize Winner *Luc Montagnier* contends that "it is the vaccination that is creating the variants."

The 2008 Nobel Laureate made his explosive comments as part of a larger interview with Pierre Barnerias of Hold-Up Media.

In April of 2020, Professor Montagnier presented a powerful case that the coronavirus was created in a lab. His comments at the time offended the left-wing establishment so much that they aggressively attempted to discredit his statement. Now, the media is backpedaling on the origin of the coronavirus after prominent scientists called for further scrutiny.

Vaccines are creating the variants

Professor Montagnier referred to the vaccine program for the coronavirus as an "unacceptable mistake." Mass vaccinations are a scientific error as well as a medical error" he said. "It is an unacceptable mistake. The history books will show that it is the vaccination that is creating the variants" Professor Montagnier continued. The prominent virologist explained that there are antibodies created by the vaccine forcing the virus to "find another solution" or die. This is where the variants are created. It is the variants that "are a production and result from the vaccination."

Antibody-dependent enhancement

Professor Montagnier said that epidemiologists know this, but are "silent" about the phenomenon, known as "Antibody-Dependent Enhancement" (ADE). In the articles that mention ADE, the concerns expressed by Professor Montagnier are dismissed saying, "Scientists say that ADE is pretty much a non-issue with COVID-19 vaccines." He explained that the trend is happening in "each country" where the "curve of vaccination is followed by the curve of deaths."

The Nobel Laureate's point is emphasized by information revealed in an open letter from a long list of medical doctors to the European Medicines Agency.

Professor Luc Montagnier continued to say that he is doing his own experiments with those who become infected with the coronavirus after getting the vaccine. "They are creating the variants that are resistant to the vaccine" he said.

Following their "Open Letter to the "Unvaccinated," an expanding group of Canadian scholars has now written a letter addressing the "the vaccinated." These writers expose the divisiveness of vaccination status and denounce the resulting rift in society.

Prime Minister Trudeau recently warned that "there will be consequences" if federal employees do not comply with vaccine mandates. This is a voice of tyranny that has reverberated fear and heightened agitation across Canada. It has launched our nation into deep division around mass vaccination and brought our collective recovery from this pandemic to a critical head. In fact, it forces us as a country, to finally ask: Indeed, what are those consequences?

What are the societal consequences of being divided along the lines of vaccination status? What are the consequences of mandating such an insufficiently tested medical intervention? How is this all supposed to end well?

The consequences will be dire, to be certain. And the consequences will affect us all, the vaccinated and the unvaccinated as well.

Over the last six months many of us made our decision to accept the vaccine in good faith—doing the right thing in order to work, travel and visit the people we love. Sadly, some of us have been pressured and coerced. And now, mounting evidence worldwide shows that these vaccines cannot stop the transmission of the virus and variants, yet vaccine mandates continue.

Meanwhile, the pharma corporations are earning billions of dollars of public money, and pushing to fast-track the vaccines towards full approval, without due process or public discussion. It is abundantly clear that when money and politics intertwine, science and ethics take a back seat.

Maybe once you resented those who hesitated to get the vaccine, as people who were not doing their part. But maybe it is time to consider that we have all become passengers on the same runaway train. The meaning of "fully vaccinated" is rapidly changing as leaders demand the next booster upgrade and threaten ousting us from public spaces if we don't comply. So, if you are among the "fully vaccinated" today, by tomorrow you may become one of the "insufficiently vaccinated" and be coerced into taking another shot.

If history is any indication, this will not stop with barring admission to concerts or bars. When you can no longer buy food, access banking, vote in person or cross a provincial border, it will be crystal clear that the same discriminatory practices that you hope to abolish will be ever more firmly established. The real consequences await all of us.

Perhaps you've had your full round of doses and are now having doubts about whether to continue based on the alarming number of infections among the vaccinated. Or maybe you know someone who has been vaccine-injured or are concerned about the mounting death reports in conjunction with vaccinations.

We keep asking ourselves, "Why is the data not allowed to be scrutinized and why are independent experts being censored if they attempt to do just that?" It is incomprehensible to see the silencing of highly regarded doctors and health scientists in our country and around the globe.

History has taught us that one-sided arguments and outlawed dissent are signs of totalitarianism lurking at the doorstep. Soon, asking questions will make you an enemy of the State. Mandating vaccines is a breaking point. "My body is my choice" has been one of the hallmarks of a free and democratic society, but this is changing. We are being robbed of personal decision making.

With lockdowns and boosters at the ready, we are entering a watershed moment. Are we all willing to continue being injected indefinitely? In Canadian provinces and around the world vaccine passports are demonstrating our "new" long-term relationship with medical coercion in exchange for basic freedoms. Thus far, each treatment has been promised to be the last, but it couldn't be clearer that there is no end in sight.

Now they're coming for our children. With extremely low risk of becoming ill and practically no risk of dying from COVID-19, the mass vaccination of children and adolescents remans unwarranted. Lining up our healthy children for medical treatment was never part of the deal. Most disturbingly of all, we are being primed for mass vaccination campaigns in our schools that do not require parental consent. Does the government decide what is best for our children? Without question, the family ties that bind us are being undone. Justifiably, parents are appalled by this unprecedented overreach and are debating pulling their children out of schools.

Despite our best intentions, families are scarred, friends are divided, and partners are at odds with each other. We have been weakened by our division and manipulated through fear.

Just how far will we allow this to go? All the way! some of us declare. But "all the way" is a place we will never reach. We need to stop this medical catastrophe and face the truth: This isn't about our health; it is about politics and it is about control.

The consequences of following current orders are greater than the threatened consequences. We entered into this for one another, not for our politicians. We have felt we have done what we have to do, and now we must say, "This is far enough, no more!"

These are the professionals who have put their names to the aforementioned:

Angela Durante, PhD, Denis Rancourt, PhD, Jan Vrbik, PhD, Laurent Leduc, PhD, Valentina Capurri, PhD, Amanda Euringer, Journalist, Claus Rinner, PhD, Maximilian C. Forte, PhD, Julie Ponesse, PhD, Michael Owen, PhD, Donald G. Welsh, PhD

Chapter 11

COVID-19 And the shadowy "Trusted News Initiative"

How it (TNI) methodically censors top world public health experts using an early warning system. The Trusted News Initiative is a partnership that includes organizations such as First Draft, Google/YouTube, Twitter, Reuters, Meta and the Washington Post. It is the only forum in the world of its kind designed to take on disinformation in real time.

By Elizabeth Woodworth — Global Research, October 22, 2021

In untangling true from false, untrained media personnel have censored the following prominent professors and researchers who have outstanding publication histories and credentials.

Dr. Jay Bhattacharya, epidemiologist, Stanford University

Dr. Sunetra Gupta, infectious disease epidemiologist, Oxford University

Dr. Martin Kulldorff, epidemiologist, Harvard

Dr. Robert Malone, inventor, of mRNA technology platform

Dr. Peter A. McCullough, former Vice-Chair Int. Med., Baylor University

Dr. Didier Raoult, microbiologist and director, IHU Mediterranee Infection; Professor at Aix Marseille University

Dr. Harvey A. Risch, Prof. Epid., Yale School of Public Health

Dr. Kurt M. Wittkowski, biometrician, 20-year head biostatistics/epid. Rockefeller University

Dr. Michael Yeadon, former VP of respiratory research, Pfizer

The TNI (Trusted News Initiative) has vigorously censored frontline physicians who have saved thousands of lives with early COVID-19 treatments: Dr. Zev Zelenko in New York, Drs. George Fareed and Brian Tyson in California; America's Frontline Doctors, founded by Dr. Simone Gold; and the Frontline COVID-19 Critical Care Alliance (FCCCA), led by ICU critical care physician Dr. Pierre Kory.

What do the inventor of mRNA technologies, The American Journal of Epidemiology, renowned epidemiologists at Harvard, Stamford and Oxford, and France's leading microbiologist have in common? They have all been censored by a repressive media network that most people have never heard of. This network has outrageously conceived and conveyed a "monopoly of legitimate information."

Exposing this uncanny censorship of eminent voices is especially vital to the fate of children and youth, who are being aggressively targeted for low-benefit, sometimes lethal, inoculations.

Since early in the COVID-19 pandemic, which according to the World Health Organization kills only 0.23% of those infected, enormous fear and panic have been fueled by the hourly drumbeat of a "one voice" media.

An international process of editorial standardization has delivered unprecedented news coverage of the monopolized message:

1. The pandemic threatens the survival of all humanity
2. There is no therapy to cure the sick
3. It is necessary to confine the whole population, and
4. The delivery will come only from a vaccine

Many people have been dismayed by the singularity of this propaganda, and how it possibly could have been achieved. That is the subject of this study.

Introduction: How the TNI Got Started

On June 24, 2021, a report from the Oxford-based Reuters Institute revealed that trust in the U.S. media—ranking last among 46 countries—had descended to an all-time low of 29%. Meanwhile, Canadian trust in media has sunk to 45%.

This downward spiral can only mean that people are going elsewhere for their news—a trend that has been accelerated by the emergence of a shadowy global censorship network called the Trusted News Initiative (TNI).

In July 2019, before the pandemic, the U.K. and Canadian governments hosted the FCO Global Conference on Media Freedom, where then BBC Director-General Tony Hall announced:

"Last month I convened, behind closed doors a Trusted News Summit at the BBC, which brought together global tech platforms and publishers. The goal was to arrive at a practical set of actions we can take together, right now, to tackle the rise of misinformation and bias... I am determined that we use a [BBC] unique reach and trusted voice to lead the way—to create a global alliance for integrity in news. We're ready to do even more to help promote freedom and democracy worldwide."

The initial Trusted News Partners in attendance were the European Broadcasting Union (EBU), Facebook, Financial Times, First Draft, Google, The Hindu and the Wall Street Journal.

This was the embryonic start of a soon-to-become a global media-wide early warning system that would rapidly alert citizens to disinformation.

Where did the idea come from?

The BBC had earlier responded to a call for evidence from the House of Lords' Select Committee on Democracy and Digital Technology, citing in its first footnote a June 3, 2019 BBC blog entitled "Tackling Misinformation."

The first point of that blog referred to a pre-pandemic March 3, 2019 BBC news report that ani-vaxxers were gaining traction on social media as part of a "fake news" movement spreading "misleading and dangerous information."

The June 3 blog also claimed a "mammoth" online scale of deceitful business practices and hate speech as problems needing "algorithmic interventions." The online "information ecosystem" was "polluted;" the size of the problem "unprecedented." The BBC and other organizations would be looking at interventions "to address misinformation across the media landscape."

Looking back at this perception of pre- COVID problems, the motives of the TNI network appear to have been constructive and reasonable. However, there was no inkling at the time of how vast, repressive, and darkly persuasive these interventions were soon to become.

The action started. CBC/Radio-Canada publicly announced its participation in the TNI in September 2019, saying "this includes a commitment to collaborate on source authentication, civic information, media education, and other responses to disinformation. The Hindu announced the Indian program simultaneously."

Two weeks after WHO announced the COVID-19 pandemic on March 11, 2020, Canada's CBC reported that the Trusted News Initiative had announced plans to "tackle coronavirus disinformation."

"Starting today, partners in the Trusted News Initiative will alert each other to disinformation about coronavirus, including 'imposter content' purporting to come from trusted sources. Such content will be reviewed promptly to ensure that disinformation is not republished."

The media partners had now expanded to include Twitter, Microsoft, Associated Press, Agence-France Presse, Reuters, and the Reuters Institute for the study of Journalism.

The TNI next agreed to engage with a new verification technology called Project Origin, led by a coalition of the BBC, CBC/-Canada, Microsoft and The New York Times—with a mandate to identify non-authorized news stories for suppression.

In July 2020, Eric Horvitz, Chief Scientific Officer for Microsoft, remarked about authorizing the news: "We've forged a close relationship with the BBC and other partners on Project Origin, aimed at methods and standards for end-to-end authentication of news and information."

By December 2020, the BBC had reported that disinformation was "spreading online to millions of people," and included minimizing COVID-19 risks along with impugning the vaccine developers' motives.

In a June 25, 2021 summary article by investigative staff, TrialSiteNews asked the question, " COVID-19 Censorship" Trusted News Initiative to Decide the Facts?" and began its reply with:

"Since time, those with power have used it to control those without. In the modern world, big government and big tech represent the seats of power when it comes to who is allowed to say what. Of course, many think that "private companies" can regulate speech in any way they see fit. But from either an ethical or legal point of view, this is false. The argument from the societal benefits of free speech works equally for posting YouTube videos and handing out flyers on a corner.

Legally, the [U.S.] Supreme Court has long held that when a private company creates something that functions as a public square (think of a company town), the First Amendment comes into play. Way back in April 2020, it was already clear that the then-existing online socio-political censorship was going to expand into the world of science, medicine, and academia in the new COVID-19 era.

What is disinformation?

This question has been sloppily handled by the mainstream media, which often confuses "misinformation" (unintentionally misleading information) with what they mean, "disinformation" which is deliberate.

Given that these definitions specify deliberate government action, it seems odd that the TNI has identified a scattered online public as the source of intentional false information and propaganda—especially concerning elections and health policy.

What are the TNI's public health sources/are they trustworthy?

The TNI reports COVID-19 health policy from the world's major public health agencies, including The World Health Organization (WHO), The U.S. Centers for Disease Control (CDC), the U.S. Food and Drug Administration (FDA), and the U.S. National Institutes of Health (NIH).

This policy is passed down through national and state governments, who convey it to the public via their media and websites, along with local case reports (based on the questionable PCR test) and deaths.

Unfortunately, this top-down leadership has at best been illogical and inconsistent, and at worst corrupted by the vast profits of the vaccine industry.

Examples of either incompetent or corrupt public health leadership include NIAID director Anthony Fauci's extraordinary contradictions concerning the protection offered by the masks.

More astonishing is the fact that on July 21, 2021, the CDC quietly recalled the use of the WHO-supported PCR test, which since February 2000 has been the global standard for measuring COVID-19 case numbers. This recall was eventually reported about a week later, yet it had appeared on the CDC website the first day after the news that George Soros and Bill Gates had acquired the U.K. COVID test company, Mologic.

The PCR test had already had a checkered history: Its recommendation had been very suddenly approved by WHO after being hurriedly rushed to publication in Eurosurveillance, one day after its submission date of January 22, 2020. Incredibly, it lacked peer review—an irregularity that was formerly challenged by 22 scientists seeking its retraction.

Worse yet, this global PCR test, which amplifies fragments of live or dead virus found in nose swabs, showed many false positives. But most shocking, if not criminal, is that the WHO, NIH, CDC and FDA have consistently denied the existence of the 85%-effective, cheap, safe and abundant early treatments for COVID.

There was to be no government-sanctioned cure until a vaccine arrived.

In spite of extensive evidence supporting early treatment efficacy and although 56 countries have adopted early treatments, there have been no TNI approved media statements that any early treatments, including hydroxychloroquine (HCQ), ivermectin (IVM), quercetin, zinc, budesonide, or Vitamins C and D, are effective in treating COVID-19 outpatients during the first 5-7 days of flu-like symptoms.

The denial has been so strong that in early 2020 many U.S. pharmacy boards—in unprecedented disrespect for the authority of physicians—banned pharmacies from filling HCQ prescriptions to treat outpatient COVID-19.

To support individual acts of censorship, the social media giants refer to the WHO, CDC, FDA, and NIH policies as their justification. Discussions such as the source of the virus, early treatments, and vaccine adverse effects—if they originate outside of these agencies—are quickly suppressed by the TNI network.

We will look at seven of these suppressions, in order of their first occurrence:

As we have seen, the medical literature is full of peer-reviewed published studies showing both the prophylactic and early treatment efficacy of a range of safe, inexpensive, readily available drugs and substances.

During the March-December 2020 period, these were claimed to be ineffective by government and the media in order to pave the way for FDA Emergency Use Authorizations for remdesivir (whose efficacy is now under question) and the mRNA vaccines.

Scandalously, hundreds of thousands of people had died while waiting for the vaccines to arrive in December 2020. Why did they die? Because their doctors were blocked from prescribing the repurposed drugs HCQ and IVM that have long been on the WHO list of essential medicines.

The TNI, by censoring the truth that the public so desperately needed, has been a primary enabler of this catastrophic, vaccine-friendly policy.

During July 2021, instead of acknowledging the early treatment evidence they had housed all along (thus being directly complicit in these deaths), the government-media complex doubled down on its intense campaign to vaccinate every one of us.

Many eminent public health professionals at the tops of their fields have stepped forward to offer sane, traditional, contagion-control measures. However, they have not been welcome in the media or the social media. TNI Director Jessica Cecil explained why, at the Trust in News conference, in April 2021.

"First, those pushing disinformation...are using apparently trustworthy sources. Anti-vax content often uses interviews with people who have medical degrees for instance.

And there is frequently a grain of truth to what is claimed. That makes untangling truth from the false harder."

The TNI also vigorously censored frontline physicians who have saved thousands of lives with early COVID-19 treatments: Dr. Zev Zelenko in New York, Drs. George Fareed and Brian Tyson in California, America's Frontline Doctors, founded by Dr. Simone Gold and the Frontline COVID-19 Critical Care Alliance (FCCCA), led by ICU/critical-care Dr. Pierre Kory.

COVID vaccine nonsense

A member of the FCCCA, Dr. Joseph Veron, who is chief of staff at United Memorial Medical Center in Houston, has more than 1,600 media interviews, yet he told local Fox reporter Ivory Hecker that reporters will never discuss his highly successful MATH+ hospital treatment protocol—"because the news producers will not allow it."

Why not? Because his hospital-based protocol using cheap, safe, plentiful drugs such as methylprednisolone, fluvoxamine, thiamine, heparin, and ivermectin, combined with zinc, ascorbic acid, and vitamin D, has yielded about half the impatient death rate reported by the CDC.

And that is not allowed by those who direct the media—those whose inferable mission is a vaccine policy based on millions of questionable PCR tests, followed by a vaccine passport that by all appearances is the endgame.

Record post-vaccine side effects and deaths have been reported online by the U.S. CDC VAERs (Vaccine Adverse Effects Reporting system), by the U.K. Yellow Card System, by the EU Vaccine Injury Reporting System, and by Israel.

In the United States VAERS reported 491,218 adverse effects and 11,405 deaths from February 10 until July 24, 2021.

However, connecting these deaths to the vaccine is not straightforward.

In England, Dr. Tess Lawrie of the Evidence-based Medicine Consultancy (EbMC), stated in June 2021 that there were at least 3 urgent questions that need to be answered by the English equivalent to CDC, the MHRA:

"How many have died within 28 days of vaccination?

How many people have been hospitalized by the vaccination?

How many people have been disabled by the vaccination?"

Also, in June, Dr. Lawrie wrote a highly-referenced 11-page letter to the MHRA Chief Executive showing that "the MHRA has more than enough evidence on the Yellow Card System to declare the COVID-19 vaccine unsafe."

Very simply put, the mRNA vaccines only generate antibodies against the single synthetic spike protein that they instruct the body first to make, and then to provide immunity against. But if the original wild SARS-2 spike mutates, the altered virus is less easily recognized by the immune system and often escapes its antibodies.

Meanwhile, natural immunity, which has fought off the whole virus and remembers it through both antibody and T-cell immunity, is much more effective—in spite of minor spike mutations.

Given the fact the world's governments and media should have allowed proof of immunity through tests such as T-Detect, which is authorized for detecting and identifying the presence of an adaptive T-Cell immune response to SARS CoV-2 in lieu of being vaccinated, for those who preferred them.

Instead, the superficially informed TNI has pushed only the highly profitable but increasingly failed experimental vaccines, which now, although they reduce risk in high-risk people, have "almost no value as a way of protecting others, so there is no benefit in vaccinating children, introducing vaccine passports domestically or internationally, or coercing young people to get a vaccine which to them is almost all risk and no benefit.

During early mRNA clinical trials, cats, ferrets, monkeys, and rabbits have experienced Antibody Dependent Enhancement (ADE) also known as pathogenic priming or a cytokine storm. This occurs when the immune system creates an overwhelming, uncontrolled inflammatory response upon being confronted with the virus in the real world, and then dies.

The Director of the Pathological Institute of the University of Heidelberg, Peter Schirmacher, has carried out over 40 autopsies on people who had died within two weeks of vaccination. Schirmacher was alarmed to cite on August 3, 2021, "rare severe side effects of the vaccination—such as cerebral vein thrombosis or autoimmune diseases."

On August 5, 2021, Israeli Dr. Kobi Haviv, at the Herzog Hospital in Jerusalem, reported that "95% of the severe patients are vaccinated ...85 to 90% of the hospitalizations are of fully vaccinated people... We are opening more and more COVID wards...The effectiveness of the vaccine is waning/fading out."

Dr. Robert Malone, inventor of mRNA technology, has explained that the susceptibility to ADE is greatest precisely during the long phase in which the vaccine tapers off: "The vaccine in its waning phase is causing the virus to replicate more efficiently than it would otherwise, which is called Antibody Dependent Enhancement," adding that all previous coronavirus vaccine development programs led to ADE.

It is essential that informed consent for COVID-19 vaccines include notification of the possibility of ADE, especially with regard to parents, whose children should be protected at all costs:

"The specific and significant COVID-19 risk of ADE should have been and should be prominently and independently disclosed to research subjects currently in vaccine trials. This is necessary in order to meet the medical ethics standard of patient comprehension for informed consent."

How many people receiving mRNA vaccines have been told this? Certainly, their Trusted News Initiative has not told them.

Only 4% of COVID deaths in England died without pre-existing conditions. In the U.S., 94.9% had pre-existing conditions.

How often have we been warned that 59% of hospital admissions are deficient in Vitamin D?

Has the government media complex ever mandated Vitamin D intake standards to take pressure off Intensive Care Units?

Has Tony Fauci ever told people to take enough Vitamin D when—according to his emails—it is an important inhibitor to contracting COVID?

Or would it have created insufficient fear to drive people to unguaranteed experimental vaccines for the TNI to let us know?

Conclusion: The Media and Democracy

A primary motive behind the formation of the TNI may have been to eradicate the so-called "disinformation."

For instance, it trusted the World Health Organization over the 2009 swine flu "pandemic" which fizzled out leaving governments to incinerate millions of dollars in vaccines.

Such industry achievements use "influencers"—falsely independent "experts," including specialist journalists, think tank facilitators, and academics whose research is funded by industry or government.

Indeed, the very function of democracy is that public wisdom should be consulted and given its head in self-rule. The public has the constitutional right to full information to form and express its own conclusions and does not need a coordinated TNI to corral and contain it.

It is utterly outrageous that those voices from the best universities are being denied us.

Perhaps the TrialSiteNews staff has said it best:

"We think that disallowing good-faith medical information because the public can't be presumed to properly weigh claims is infantilizing said public, along with dismantling the free speech culture that perhaps peaked in the 20th Century. The efforts now underway to completely suppress positive data associated with early-onset treatments such as Ivermectin, or the squelching of any discussion of vaccine safety is completely unacceptable. In a civilized, democratic market-based society, those perpetuating such offenses are in fact on the wrong side of history."

Chapter 12

By Lance Johnson—September 3, 2021

Israel had more COVID Infections per capita than any country in the world even as booster shots were being widely administered there.

Just a few months ago the mainstream media praised Israel for its "pandemic ending" vaccination campaign. With over 40 percent of the population "fully vaccinated" in the first quarter of 2021, Israel was well on its way to stopping community spread and clearing its hospitals.

However, the nation of Israel imposed some of the strictest lockdowns during that time, segregating the unvaccinated from public life. Israel brought up the Pfizer/BioNTech mRNA COVID vaccine and began issuing mandatory Green Pass "vaccine passports" as a requirement for citizens to enter public spaces. By August, Israel had intimidated and coerced its population into having one of the highest vaccination rates in the world, with 78% percent of people 12 years of age and older classified as "fully vaccinated."

The world was reassured that this rate of vaccination was more than enough to ensure individual and "herd immunity." However, infection rates have skyrocketed across the country since then, and Israel is now logging the world's highest infection rates, with nearly 650 new cases daily per million people. At times hospitalizations for the "fully vaccinated " have reached upward of 95 percent.

Pfizer/BioNTech vaccine is failing Israel, with case load and hospitalizations climbing in the vaccinated.

By August 15, there were 514 Israelis hospitalized with severe COVID-19, a 31 percent increase from just four days earlier. Most of the hospitalized patients had already received at least one vaccine and 59 percent were fully vaccinated.

The Isreali people's committee report, malfuctions, failures and damages

"There are so many breakthrough infections that most of the hospitalized patients are actually vaccinated" said Uri Shalit, a bio-informatician at the Israel Institute of Technology. The vaccines do not protect older populations either—a false promise advertised since the beginning of the vaccine rollout. In fact, of the hospitalized vaccinated patients, 87 percent were 60 or older.

This has not stopped the Israeli government from tripling down with this vaccine program. Israeli officials have already begun to administer a third dose of the failed Pfizer vaccine to the population. Now controlled by the Green Pass vaccine passport system, Israelis are lining up to be vaccinated again. More than 100,000 booster shots are being administered each day, with 2.15 million Israelis having received their third shot.

Despite compounding vaccination, the nation still suffers, with the world's worst seven-day rolling average number of COVID cases per capita. Israel is on track to pass 11,000 daily COVID cases—an infection rate that is magnitudes higher than a year before, when everyone in the country was unvaccinated. U.S. health officials have access to this data, but were quick to approve the Pfizer/BioNTech vaccine and begin pushing for unlawful vaccine mandates across the country.

Using a non-neutralizing vaccine against a novel, endemic virus only perpetuates the transmissibility of the virus among people. When the spike protein of that virus is forcibly replicated throughout the population, entirely new health problems occur. By placing selective pressure on an amino acid sequence leads to new outbreaks and vaccine failure. A study published in the Journal of Infection discusses antibody dependent enhancement and the serious risks of the vaccine program. Any perceived benefits of vaccination for coronaviruses are short-lived, as artificially augmented antibody levels wane, making the population more susceptible.

Now living in a medical police state, Israelis who were suddenly considered "unvaccinated" were banned from public spaces if they hadn't submitted to a THIRD dose of Pfizer's spike protein mRNA.

Chapter 13

By Arsenio Toledo — 9/3/21

Fauci says government on track to administer COVID-19 Booster doses every eight months

Chief Medical Advisor to the White House Dr. Anthony Fauci said the United States is on track to administer Wuhan coronavirus (COVID-19) vaccine booster doses every eight months.

On Sunday, August 29, Fauci appeared on the program of mainstream media outlet, "Meet the Press." He claimed that the federal government is strongly considering providing COVID-19 booster doses to Americans eight months after they get their last dose of the vaccine. It is interesting to note that scientists warn that the push for COVID-19 booster shots is not based on scientific data but is based on politics and profits which is what is driving the vaccine policies.

But the after intervention of President Joe Biden, Fauci agreed that the government could be "flexible" about this issue. While the plan would not change right now, it could be amended soon based on the "data."

"We're still planning on eight months," said Fauci to "Meet the Press" host Chuck Todd. "That was the calculation we made."

But Fauci added that the country's public health authorities are "open to any variation" of this timetable "based on the data."

Later on, in the interview, Fauci admitted that the COVID-19 vaccines available in the U.S. are not very effective. He did this by admitting that he was certain the Pfizer and Moderna vaccines require a third dose, while the Johnson & Johnson vaccine did not.

"We were dealing, Chuck, with a totally emergency situation," said Fauci. "If we had the grace to be able to do this in a very slow, measured manner, the phase-two study would have given various intervals of dosing."

It is entirely conceivable that when all is said and done the standard regime will be a three-dose shot for [Pfizer and Moderna] and a two-dose shot for Johnson & Johnson.

Fauci tried to rationalize this sudden change by claiming that the country leaders' priorities are saving lives and not providing the country with accurate data regarding the COVID-19 vaccines.

"We were having to save lives and we needed to do it very quickly. So, I don't think there was anything errant or wrong in the way we started it with two doses," he said. "But at least now we're being very open and flexible that we may need that third dose."

Biden pushing Fauci to require booster COVID-19 doses

Fauci and other public health officials have outlined a schedule for administering additional COVID-19 doses. Biden has publicly asked these officials if the gap between the booster doses could be shortened. He did this after a visit by the Israeli prime minister.

On Friday, August 27, Biden met with Israeli Prime Minister Naftali Bennett at the White House. After receiving advice from the prime minister, Biden asked his health officials to consider if following Israeli's timetable regarding the administering of booster doses is viable.

"We're considering the advice you've given that we should start earlier," said Biden to Bennett. "Should it be as little as five months? That's being discussed."

It should be noted that Israel, one of the world's most vaccinated countries with 60% of its population fully vaccinated, is dealing with a massive post-vaccine COVID-19 outbreak. The country recently passed one million total COVID-19 cases, with nearly 11,000 Israelis testing positive.

Israel also has over 83,000 active COVID-19 cases, and over 7,000 people have died of COVID-19 over there.

The booster doses would have to be first approved by the Food and Drug Administration and the Advisory Committee on Immunization Practices. The latter is a committee within the Centers for Disease Control and Prevention that advises vaccination policies.

The push by so-called public health experts and leading Democrats to mandate COVID-19 booster doses has been strongly criticized by many conservatives and republicans. Notably, former President Trump called the plan a "money-making operation" by Pfizer.

Chapter 14

J.D. Heyes a seasoned writer, journalist and columnist writes as follows:

Joe Biden's military has ordered all personnel to get a COVID-19 vaccine or face disciplinary action that would include removal from their service branch, but two members who have already had the virus and have natural immunity are bucking what they view as an unlawful order and are fighting back, in court.

According to the Children's Defense Fund, the two members have filed legal action on behalf of themselves and the other 220,000 personnel who have already had the illness and now have natural immunity, a suit that comes on the heels of new research proving that natural immunity works best to fend off even the delta variant better than any of the three approved vaccines.

"The lead plaintiffs in the lawsuit, Staff Sergeant Daniel Robert and Staff Sergeant Holli Mulvihill, allege U.S. Sec of Defense Lloyd Austin ignored the DOD's own regulations and created an entirely new definition of 'full immunity' as being achievable only by vaccination," the organizations reports in a press release.

"According to the law suit, the military's existing laws and regulations unequivocally provide the exemption the plaintiffs seek under Army Regulation 40-562 ('AR 40-562'), which provides documented survivors of an infection a presumptive medical exemption from vaccination because of the natural immunity acquired as a result of having survived the infection," the release continues.

Specifically, that section of Army Regulations reads:

General examples of medical exemptions include the following . . . Evidence of immunity based on serologic tests, documented infection or similar circumstances.

So, it seems that, on the surface, certainly, the Pentagon has violated its own regulations by ordering all Army personnel, at least, to get vaccinated even if they've recovered from the coronavirus, not to mention putting all service members in danger.

The lawsuit notes that retired Adm. Brett Giroir, a pediatrician and the former assistant secretary for Health and Human Services, noted in an August 24 interview with Fox News that "natural immunity, is very important."

"There is still no data to suggest vaccine immunity is better than natural immunity," he continued, adding: "I think both are highly protective."

But no matter; Defense Secretary Lloyd Austin, a former defense contractor executive and retired four-start Army general, followed his orders and issued a directive that all of the U.S. armed forces would have to be vaccinated.

And he wrote specifically, "Those with previous COVID-19 infection are not considered fully vaccinated."

So, in other words, the Biden regime doesn't really care about "the science"—it cares about feeding big Pharma.

The plaintiffs also allege in their lawsuit that Austin, who has no medical training, and is not a physician, changed the Defense Department's regulation without giving a "scintilla of evidence to support" the altercation.

Robert F. Kennedy, Jr.:

"Natural immunity appears to confer longer lasting plus stronger protection against SARS-CoV-2 infection, symptomatic disease and hospitalization from the Delta variant compared to Pfizer-BioNTech's two-dose vaccine-induced immunity. They also say that the defense secretary made the change to the regulation without subjecting it to the normal rule making process, which violates the Administrative Procedures Act.

What's more, even though the Food and Drug Administration has 'approved' these still-experimental vaccines, Pfizer's phase 3 trials, which aim to measure long-term side effects, are not supposed to be completed until 2023."

Mary Holland, president and general counsel of Children's Health Defense, lauded the lead plaintiffs for filing suit against the military's mandate.

"They raise critical issues that courts must resolve—on medical exemptions for natural immunity, and whether the clinical trials serving as the basis for Pfizer's licensure were sufficient," said Holland.

Chapter 15

By Nolan Barton

Nolan Barton & Olmos, LLP is a Silicon Valley law firm devoted exclusively to advising and representing individuals and corporations accused of crimes. "We are an AV-rated firm and are listed in the Preeminent Edition of Martindale Hubbell. The firm takes pride in providing high quality representation tailored to our clients' individual needs and resources."

Top FDA vaccine regulators resign in frustration as Biden administration oversteps mandate and pushes risky, unproved booster shots

Two of the most senior leaders in vaccine regulations at the Food and Drug Administration (FDA) are set to leave their positions as the Biden administration continues to overstep the mandate of the agency.

Marion Gruber, director of the Office of Vaccines Research and Review (OVRR) plans to retire in October and Deputy Director Phil Kraus who has been at the FDA for more than a decade has announced that he too will be leaving the agency.

OVRR is part of the FDA's Center for Biologics Evaluation and Research (CBER).

The pair of announcements came barely a week after the FDA granted full approval to Pfizer's coronavirus (COVID-19) vaccine as the Biden administration intensified its push for booster doses. (Related: Biden pushes third spike protein "booster" injection on Americans).

Gruber, Krause not happy with Biden's authoritarian vaccine regime

In a memo CBER (Center for Biologics Evaluation and Research) director Peter Marks said he will serve as the acting director of the OVRR (Office of Vaccines Research and Review) while the FDA searches for its next director. The search process will begin immediately, he said. The memo did not give a reason for Gruber's or Krause's departure, but there were reports that they were not happy with the Biden administration's authoritarian COVID-19 vaccine regime.

A former senior FDA leader told independent news organization Endpoints that the two were leaving because they're frustrated that the Centers for Disease Control and Prevention (CDC) and its Advisory Committee on Immunization Practices (ACIP) are involved in decisions they think should be up to the FDA.

The former FDA official also said he's heard they're upset with Marks for not insisting that those decisions should be kept inside the FDA. He added that the last straw was the White House getting ahead of the FDA on booster doses.

The Biden administration apparently finds ACIP more amenable to its vaccine agenda.

Just recently, the administration jumped ahead of the FDA's reviews of booster doses and announced that they might be available by the week of September 20. With the COVID-19 vaccines appearing to fail against variants of the virus, it remains unclear what benefits an additional dose would provide.

Public health experts oppose rollout of boosters

More and more public health experts are opposing the rollout of the boosters. Some are recommending that the virus be allowed to circulate throughout the population, with precautions taken for vulnerable individuals.

"We really cannot do anything else but allow the virus to take its course in order for the population to achieve "herd" immunity," said Porolfur Gudnason, chief epidemiologist of Iceland's Directorate of Health. "We need to try to vaccinate and better protect those who are vulnerable, but let us tolerate the infection. It is not a priority now to vaccinate everyone with the third dose."

Chapter 16

Paul Craig Roberts, is an American Economist and author

"The massive outbreak of new COVID cases in the most vaccinated countries—Israel 84%, Iceland 95%, Gibraltar 99%, has made it completely clear that the mRNA vaccine has had minimal protection against the COVID infection. Fauci, a lifelong shill for Big Pharma, is delighted. His solution to the failure of the "vaccine" (it is not a vaccine) is that booster shots are needed; he says, every 5 to 8 months to keep COVID at bay. In other words, profits forever for Big Pharma.

In other words it is safe to say that the vaccine has had little effect in protecting against COVID.

This is the conclusion of a number of top scientists and medical authorities who are far superior in their knowledge than Big Pharma and the completely ignorant American media who keep repeating "a pandemic of the unvaccinated" when the outbreaks are centered among the vaccinated in the most vaccinated countries.

We have to ask if it is possible for American journalists to be as stupid as they present themselves to be, or are they being paid to lie? We know that Fauci and Walensky benefit from vaccine profits. Somehow, this conflict of interest does not enter public discussion.

Indeed, all facts are censored, suppressed, and kept out of public discussion. That is the function of "mainstream media," CNN, NPR, New York Times, Washington Post, and the rest of the media.

The "COVID crisis" is from start to finish a manufactured crisis. The purpose of the mRNA may well have worsened the crisis, which will lead to more counterproductive measures that threaten not merely freedom, but life itself.

It has been proven in India and Africa that Ivermectin used as a preventative for COVID outbreaks, and Ivermectin has been proven as a cure by the success of many doctors who have used Ivermectin to cure their patients of COVID. Ivermectin is a safe and effective cure.

If you need more evidence of Ivermectin's effectiveness, the Chairman of the Tokyo Medical Association announced in a press conference that Ivermectin is a safe and effective treatment for COVID and recommends that all doctors begin using Ivermectin to treat COVID patients.

Yet Western public medical authorities (not Japanese, Indian, and African) and the media continue to lie through their teeth that Ivermectin is unsafe. Do they tell this lie just for profits, or is there a darker agenda afoot?

HCQ is another proven preventative and cure and it is also demonized as dangerous. HCQ needs to be taken early when symptoms first appear. Ivermectin is effective also at later stages of the virus.

If you came down with COVID and had co-morbidities or a compromised immune system, a hospital would put you on a ventilator. You would not get treatment with known safe and effective cures. In Japan, or India, and any of the African countries or in Mexico, you could purchase Ivermectin fvormulated for humans over the counter from a pharmacy. In the U.S. it's best to try to get in contact with Frontline Doctors who are overwhelmed with pleas for help from americans.

It is only in English speaking countries, the U.S., Western Europe, and in Israel that the population is unable to get safe and effective treatment for COVID infection. Israel is advocating a 4th booster shot of the identical vaccine that has filled its hospitals with fully vaccinated patients. In the U.S. Fauci says it will be booster shots every 8 months. This means endless adverse reactions to the "vaccine" and endless appearance of new "variants." It also means endless profits for Big Pharma, and that is all that is important.

The COVID policy being implemented in the West has no logic and no basis in any known facts. What is going on?

Doctors and scientists have reported the effectiveness of HCQ and Ivermectin, which have such safe records of use over decades that in countries not controlled by pharmaceutical companies are available for over-the-counter purchase just like aspirin. Yet the corrupt American medical establishment declares the proven preventatives and cures are "unsafe," and the mRNA vaccine that is spreading COVID is declared to be the answer.

What is the agenda? Clearly it is not the health of the public. Obviously, they want more variants, more COVID cases, more deaths and health injuries with which to scare the sheep, sell more vaccine, and impose more violations of civil liberty.

How can it be that in "free and democratic America" truth and facts are excluded from the discussion and have no impact on COVID policy? How can it be that the leading scientists and medical practitioners who issue warnings against the growing vaccine catastrophe are censored and threatened with losing their medical licenses and employment?

What is happening today in America, Canada, Western Europe, Australia and New Zealand? Real experts were discredited, and in their place, we have CNN and other Big Pharma shills.

How can it be that in the midst of COVID infection, disinformation is intentionally spread online by such sites as Coronavirus World Updates? In my opinion, Coronavirus World

PANDEMIC PANDEMONIUM

Updates is an Internet lie sheet sponsored by green-driven Big Pharma for the purpose of spreading disinformation in order to discourage people from seeking out and obtaining effective treatment for COVID infection.

A fake story from a disinformation site was picked up from Rolling Stones magazine about the danger of Ivermectin, one of the safest medicines known, taken weekly in most of Africa as a preventative and treatment for River Blindness. The dishonest article, which had to be retracted, quoted a doctor who blamed Ivermectin for people overdosing themselves by taking dosages formulated for large animals such as horses. It turns out that the doctor made up the entire story.

People cannot get safe and effective treatment for COVID, because an incompetent and corrupt medical system will only vaccinate, refuses to treat COVID infection with appropriate doses of HCQ or Ivermectin, spreads fake stories to scare people away from successful treatment, and seeks to take away medical licenses of the doctors who are actually saving lives. One wonders if the doctor was paid by Big Pharma for his fake story. It wasn't only the Rolling Stone and Coronavirus World Updates that reported the story. The entirety of the presstitute media was involved.

Why do the the media work with Big Pharma to deceive people, prevent them from safe treatment, causing death and injury to large numbers of people? Here is Big Pharma setting you up for booster shots.

Is it incompetence or evil that rises from the American Medical professionals and it's presstitute shills? If "our medical authorities" don't succeed in stamping out our lives with the mRNA vaccine, they obviously have something else waiting to unleash to do the job.

Healthy people face miniscule threat of death or serious injury from COVID. Vulnerable people with co-morbidities can be safely and securely put on preventative doses of Ivermectin and HCQ. There is no reason, other than pure negligence of the medical profession which withholds treatment with known cures."

Chapter 17

By Dr. Rudolf Hansel, author at Global Research

Dear Friends and esteemed colleagues!

The future of our culture will largely depend on whether there will be enough free thinkers to enlighten us about what is truth and what is a lie. This requires an independent mind, which is in nobody's service, a high degree of common sense and the moral consciousness to be his brother's keeper.

The greater the courage of a thinker, the more he dares to question, the less he/she conforms to the crowd. His thinking is not just mind games; thinking he changes the world. He is the type of an honest spirit, an ethicist and true human being who takes responsibility for himself and all other human beings (thinking). With the freedom of thinking, freedom in general is proclaimed. For truth is not an end in itself, it is merely the mold for something greater, namely freedom. Truth alone can make us free. The intellectual therefore has a much greater responsibility than one would commonly like to admit.

At the same time, a free thinker will never claim to have the only blessed truth. For the free mind, there is an unlimited number of truths to be discovered and to follow change. For him, truth is not that which is dogmatic and does not divide people into believers and non-believers or those of other faiths, but which is beneficial to the coexistence of people and promotes their understanding and common sense.

Since every individual is needed to shape the future, we cannot wait for a Messiah. Action must be taken here and now. Therefore, I see the only non-violent way is to continue to enlighten, to convey hope and never give up. Killing arguments like "conspiracy theorist" or "fascist" should not unsettle free spirits. Undecided people have to be picked up in a friendly and understanding way from where they are at the moment.

If, for example, fellow citizens assume that the politicians want to protect the health of the population by prescribing coercive measures such as lockdown, quarantine or muzzling, then it should be conveyed to him that the levels of power were already occupied years ago by corrupt, immoral, petty and mendacious political actors because they willingly implemented the orders of the ruling psychopaths. These lackeys must one day step down. Evil will not triumph because man, though irritated, is good and social by nature.

If anyone thinks in connection with the prescribed political coercive measures and the upcoming compulsory vaccination, that politicians and citizens would be well advised to trust the expert opinions of medical practitioners of all stripes, then they should be reminded that no profession was as deeply involved as the German Nazis as doctors. In a sense, they formed the backbone of the German Nazi crimes.

If fellow citizens do not know or do not want to admit that free countries and free governments are being deliberately destroyed by unscrupulous great powers and that the public is being deceived about this, then they are advised to read John Pilger's article in "Global Research" about the decades of suffering of the Afghan people. "The Great Game of Breaking Up Countries." The award-winning journalist pleads for taking the truth about the past seriously so that all this suffering never happens again. Yet Afghanistan is only one of many examples of the brutal campaigns of conquest and economic warfare of the empire.

PANDEMIC PANDEMONIUM

If fellow human beings hope that the current crimes against humanity will soon come to an end, then they should be gently prepared for the fact that subsequent coercive measures are already planned to curb the allegedly man-made climate change. At the same time, they should be given hope as more and more people around the world are waking up and standing up against the gigantic hoax and crimes.

If a fellow citizen finds himself in a seemingly hopeless economic, financial and social plight because of the inhuman machinations of the authorities, then he is strongly advised to turn to fellow human beings, because of the principle of "mutual aid" as well as social feelings and communal bonds play just as great a role in the human world as the will to power and self-interest.

But if anyone wants to drive fellow human beings to revolt against the power of the state, then they must be strongly advised not to do so, because the power of the state is well armed and the blood and freedom of others must be treated with care.

Chapter 18

Brian Shilhavy is the founder and owner of Healthy Traditions, Inc. He is also the Managing Editor, Founder and owner of Health Impact News.

The battle lines over mandatory COVID-19 vaccines are now going full steam ahead in the U.S. as the Biden Administration is announcing today that all federal employees must now get a COVID-19 shot as a condition for employment, and that they are eliminating the testing opt-out.

The argument that only COVID-19 will end the "endless" pandemic and the lie that hospitals are over 90% full of unvaccinated people are being used as justification for mandatory mass vaccination.

It doesn't take much research or one's own to bypass the corporate media and find out that they are lying and that there are numerous reports that the exact opposite situation is now happening in the U.S. and around the world, which is that the hospitals are full of people who have already been vaccinated with COVID-19 shots and that the ones who have survived are now filling our hospitals.

This is evident from the last release of data into the government Vaccine Event Reporting System (VAERS) database, which as of last Friday shows that following COVID-19 shots, there have been 13,911 deaths, 18,098 permanent disabilities, 76,160 ER visits, 56,912 hospitalizations, 2,933,377 injury symptoms, and 14,327 life threatening events.

These are just the cases that have been reported and that the CDC has allowed to be released to the public. Many healthcare workers have stated that there is pressure from doctors and hospital administrations to NOT relate injuries to the COVID-19 shots and to not report them in VAERS, which one nurse stated takes over 30 minutes to do for a single case and is very time consuming.

We have previously exposed government's lies on who it is filling the hospitals today.

Insanity rules the U.S. as hospitalizations and deaths among vaccinated cases surge while health authorities blame the unvaccinated.

And just this past week the Toronto Sun ran a story reporting that more than 100 Ontario youth were sent to the hospital for vaccine-related heart problems.

A report quietly released last week by Public Health Ontario (PHO) tallies the number of people in the province admitted to the hospital with heart inflammation following the mRNA vaccination and it skews heavily towards young people.

As of August 7, 2021, there were 106 incidents of myocarditis/pericarditis in Ontarians under the age of 25. That is slightly more than half of the total of all such incidents."

Surgical Neurology International, April, 2022

By Dr. Russell Blaylock

The COVID pandemic is one of the most manipulated infectious disease events in history, characterized by the official lies in unending stream lead by government bureaucracies, medical associations, medical boards, the media and international agencies

For the first time in American history a president, governors, mayors, hospital administrators and federal bureaucrats are determining medical treatments based not on accurate science, but rather to force the acceptance of special forms of care and prevention using respirators and untested mRNA vaccines.

For the first time in history medical treatment protocols are not being formulated based on the experience of the physicians treating the largest number of patients successfully, but rather individuals and bureaucracies that have never treated a single patient including Anthony Fauci, Bill Gates, EcoHealth Alliance, the CDC, WHO, state public health officers and hospital administrators.

The media (TV, newspapers, magazines, etc.) medical societies, state medical boards and the owners of social media have appointed themselves to be the sole source of information concerning this so-called "pandemic."

Websites have been removed, highly credentialed and experienced clinical doctors and scientific experts in the field of infectious diseases have been demonized, careers have been destroyed and all dissenting information has been labeled "misinformation" and "dangerous lies", even when sourced from top experts in fields of virology, infectious diseases, pulmonary critical care and epidemiology.

These blackouts of truth occur even when this information is backed by extensive scientific citations from some of the most qualified medical specialists in the world. Incredibly, even individuals such as Dr. Michael Yeadon, a retired ex-Chief Scientist, and vice-president for the science division of Pfizer Pharmaceutical company in the U.K. is ignored and demonized.

Dr. Peter McCullogh, one of the most cited experts in his field, has successfully treated over 2000 patients by using a protocol of early treatment (which the so-called experts completely ignored). He has published his results in peer reviewed journals, reporting an 80% reduction in hospitalizations and a 75% reduction in deaths by using an early treatment. Despite this, he is under an unrelenting series of attacks by the information controllers, none of which have treated a single patient.

Other unprecedented attacks

Another unprecedented tactic is to remove dissenting doctors from their position as journal editors, reviewers and retracting of the scientific papers from journals, even after these papers have been in print. Until this pandemic event, I have never seen so many journal papers being retracted — the vast majority promoting alternatives to official dogma, especially if the papers question vaccine safety. Normally, a submitted paper or study is reviewed by experts in the field, called peer review. These reviews can be quite intense and nit picking in detail, insisting that all errors within the paper be corrected before publication. So, unless fraud or some other major hidden problem is discovered after the paper is in print, the paper remains in the scientific literature.

We are now witnessing a growing number of excellent scientific papers, written by top experts in the field, being retracted from major medical and scientific journals weeks, months and even years after publication. A careful review indicates that in far too many instances the authors dared question accepted dogma by the controllers of scientific publications — especially concerning the safety, alternative treatments or efficacy of vaccines. These journals rely on extensive advertising by pharmaceutical companies for their review. Several instances have occurred where powerful pharmaceutical companies exerted their influence on owners of these journals to remove articles that in any way question these companies' products.

As concerns the information made available to the public, virtually all the media is under the control of these pharmaceutic giants or others who are benefitting from this "pandemic." Their stories are all the same, both in content and even wording. Orchestrated coverups occur daily and massive data exposing the lies being generated by these information controllers are hidden from the public. All data coming over the national media (TV, newspaper and magazines), as well as the local news you watch every day, comes from "official" sources—most of which are lies, distortions or completely manufactured out of the whole cloth—all aimed to deceive the public.

While these attacks on free speech is terrifying enough, even worse is the virtually universal control hospital administrators have exercised over the details of medical care in hospitals. These hirelings are now instructing doctors which treatment protocols they will adhere to and which treatments they will not use, no matter how harmful the "approved" treatments are or how beneficial the "unapproved" are.

The draconian measures established to contain this "contrived" pandemic have never been shown to be successful, such as masking the public, lockdowns, and social distancing. A number of carefully done studies during previous flu seasons demonstrated that masks, of any kind, had never prevented the spread of the virus among the public.

In fact, some very good studies suggested that masks actually spread the virus by giving people a false sense of security and other factors, such as the observation that people were constantly breaking sterile technique by touching their mask, improper removal and by leakage of infectious aerosols around the edges of the mask. In addition, masks were being disposed of in parking lots, walking trails, laid on tabletops in restaurants and placed in pockets or purses.

Within a few minutes of putting on a mask, a number of pathogenic bacteria can be cultured from the masks, putting the immune suppressed person at high risk of bacterial pneumonia and children at a higher risk of meningitis. A study by researchers at the University of Florida cultured over 11 pathogenic bacteria from the inside of the mask worn by children in schools.

PANDEMIC PANDEMONIUM

It was also known that children were at essentially no risk of getting sick from the virus or transmitting it.

In addition, it was also known that wearing a mask for over 4 hours (as occurs in all schools) results in significant hypoxia (low blood oxygen levels) and hypercapnia (high CO_2 levels), which have a number of deleterious effects on health, including impairing the development of the child's brain.

Chapter 19

U.S. News—Sept. 10, 2021

Republican governors threaten lawsuits over Biden's coronavirus vaccine mandates

Republican Governors are threatening legal action following President Biden's sweeping vaccine requirement announcement this week.

The GOP particularly took issue with the Biden administration's move to develop a rule to require private sector companies with more than 100 employees to ensure workers get vaccinated against the coronavirus or face weekly testing before going to work. The White House estimated that the rule would affect 80 million workers.

"I will pursue every legal option available to the state of Georgia to stop this blatantly unlawful overreach by the Biden administration," Georgia Gov. Brian Kemp tweeted.

Texas Gov. Greg Abbott called the coming rule an "assault on private businesses," adding that "Texas is already working to halt this power grab."

South Dakota Gov. Kristi Noem tweeted that her state will "stand up to defend freedom," adding to Biden, "see you in court."

Nebraska Gov. Pete Ricketts in a statement called the measure a "stunning violation of personal freedom and abuse of the federal government's power."

The announcement also drew attention from the Republican National Committee. RNC Chairwoman Ronna McDaniel described the rule as "unconstitutional" and said the group "will sue the administration to protect Americans and their liberties." But Biden welcomed the challenges. When asked about potential legal action against the rule on Friday, he said, "Have at it."

"We're playing for real here," Biden told reporters. "This isn't a game."

Biden in his Thursday speech called out elected officials who are "actively working to undermine the fight against COVID-19" without specifically naming anyone, though the president has butted heads with several GOP governors on coronavirus-related mitigation measures.

Sept. 12, 2021

Fox News's Sean Hannity took on President Biden over the new vaccine mandates, saying the president needs to stay out of other people's health decisions.

"You better get the vaccine, or Dr. Joe Biden is going to unleash the full force of the federal government against you," Hannity said on his show Friday Mediaite reported.

Biden announced Thursday new vaccine mandates for the country, telling employers with more than 100 employees they must either get their employees fully vaccinated or require weekly testing.

"It doesn't matter if you prefer to keep your medical decisions private," Hannity said.

Hannity encouraged his viewers back in July to "take COVID seriously" and said he believed in the science of vaccination."

However, many Republicans who support the coronavirus vaccine came out vigorously against the vaccine mandates.

Hannity went after Biden for not having vaccine mandates on "illegal aliens" but instead going after American citizens who don't get the vaccine. He called the vaccine mandate "deeply unconstitutional."

Republican governors and others have vowed to fight the federal government's vaccine mandate in court, with Biden telling the challengers to "have at it."

Chapter 20

Employers are uniting and preparing lawsuits against Biden's seditious vaccine and testing mandates

By Lance D. Johnson — Writer and Freelance Journalist

The Biden regime continues to declare war on the American People. On September 9, 2021, Biden gave one of the most outlandish speeches in American history, while espousing a number of unconstitutional decrees that violate the sanctity of the individual and the free market. In the speech, Biden demanded all businesses with more than 100 employees to violate the medical privacy and body autonomy of all their employees, and require injections. Under Biden's decree, employees who do not comply will be stripped of their due process rights, classified as vectors of disease, and subject to weekly COVID-19 test swabs and/or nasal probes are provably fraudulent.

Private employees banding together against tyranny waged by the federal government

Private Employers across the country are banding together and preparing historic lawsuits against Biden's seditious vaccine mandate. Charlie Kirk from Turning Point USA, tweeted out, "Mandating vaccines for our 170 plus full-time employees at Turning Point USA? No chance. We will sue you Joe Biden, and win.

Angelina Morabito, spokeswoman for Campus Reform, tweeted that Biden's sweeping mandate will be challenged by millions of companies. "If you listen really closely to the livestream of Biden's speech, you can hear the sound of a million lawsuits being filed" she wrote.

Kansas Sen. Dr. Roger Marshall, called the mandate an all-out assault on private business, our civil liberties, and our entire constitutional system of limited government. This will likely get struck down in the court."

Every adult has already been given access for the experimental vaccines, which are predictably causing waning immune responses. The remaining Americans are either at low risk to the advertised infection and can readily garner immunity or they already have natural immunity that is comprehensive and durable. In all cases, people need to be left alone to their private medical decisions and treated fairly, and the doubly vaccinated need to realize that they will be required to get yearly boosters (or more) if they go along with this.

Desantis makes Florida an outliner on vaccines for young children

By: Cecelia Smith-Schoenwalder — June 17, 2022

Florida Gov. Ron DeSantis this week distanced his state from the Biden administration's efforts to vaccinate young children against COVID-19, calling the Government's plans a "convoluted vaccine distribution process."

The Republic governor said that no state resources will be dedicated to getting children under 5 the shots in a decision that amplifies continuing disagreements DeSantis and President Joe Biden.

"There is not going to be any state programs that are going to be trying to get COVID jabs to infants and toddlers and newborns," DeSantis said in a press conference on Thursday. "That's not something that we think is appropriate, so that's not where we are going to be utilizing our assets."

White House Press Secretary Karine Jean-Pierre on Thursday confirmed that Florida was the only state that did not pre-order shots for the age group made available by the Biden administration.

"By being the only state not pre-ordering, pediatricians for example, in Florida will not have immediate access to the vaccines" Jean-Pierre said. "Some pharmacies and community health centers in the state get access through federal distribution channels, but those options are limited for parents."

The Florida Department of Health defended the decision, adding that doctors could still order the shots on their own.

The Department in March became the only state to recommend against COVID-19 vaccination for healthy children ages 5-11."

"Our Department of Health has been very clear, the risk outweighs the benefits and we recommend against it," said DeSantis, who has emerged as a possible candidate in the 2024 presidential election. "That's not the same as banning it. People can access it if they want to.

The Biden administration made 10 million shots available to states to pre-order. The Food and Drug Administration on Friday granted emergency use authorization to the shots from Pfizer and Moderna. Before shots can begin, experts from the Centers for Disease Control and Prevention as well as the director must recommend the vaccines. The CDC's vaccine advisory group is scheduled to vote on the recommendation Saturday afternoon, while the director's endorsement is expected soon after.

Chapter 21

Twilight's last gleaming. Biden's so-called vaccine mandates.

By Judge Andrew P. Napolitano

Judge Napolitano served as a New Jersey Superior Court judge from 1987—1995. He was a visiting professor at Brooklyn Law School. His education is from Notre Dame Law School and Princeton University.

"This is not about freedom or personal choice." —*President Joseph R. Biden—Sept. 9, 2021*

It was scandalous and infuriating to hear President Biden argue last week that his so-called vaccine mandates somehow have nothing to do with freedom or personal choice. In saying that, he has rejected our history, our values and the Constitution he swore to uphold.

He made his ignorant statement while outlining his plan to have the Department of Labor issue emergency regulations requiring every employer in America of 100 or more persons to compel all its employees to receive a vaccine against COVID-19, or the employer will be fined.

He claims the authority to issue these orders under the 1970 Occupational Safety and Health Act, or OSHA. Though it has been around for 51 years, OSHA is profoundly unconstitutional, as it purports to authorize federal bureaucrats to regulate private workplace property unavailable to the public.

Congress enacted this legislation relying on its Commerce Clause power in the Constitution. But the Commerce Clause—according to James Madison, who wrote it, only empowers Congress to keep commerce regular; it does not empower Congress to regulate the conditions of production of goods and service intended for commerce.

However, notwithstanding the plain language of the Commerce Clause—"Congress shall have power. . . to regulate Commerce . . . among several States"—the Supreme Court, since the era of President Franklin D. Roosevelt which has given Congress a blank check authorizing it to regulate anything that affects commerce. Congress has used this clause to justify its vast expansions of federal power more than it has used any other clause in the Constitution.

Nevertheless, there is no authority for federal workplace regulation in the Constitution, as it was reserved to the states by the 10th Amendment. That Amendment declares that the states kept for themselves that which they did not delegate to the feds.

Freedom in the time of COVID-19

The Ninth Amendment underscores that we have many personal rights not enumerated in the Constitution or the Bill of Rights and the government is required to respect them. After the right to live, ownership and control of your own body are foremost among those unenumerated rights.

The President, like all of us, is subject to the laws of nature and is obliged to recognize the natural law. It posits that our rights come from our humanity, and not from the government. It was with the natural law in mind that Madison authored the Ninth Amendment and its protection of unenumerated rights.

If self-ownership is not among those rights, then nothing is. If the government owns our bodies, or somehow can trump our personal ownership of them, then we have no rights.

Every state permits a sick person to reject medication. Biden not only rejects that right, but he rejects the right of healthy persons to decline an experimental vaccine.

What's going on here?

Does the government work for us, or do we work for the government?

Such a question would have been laughable 100 years ago. But today, the government treats us as if we work for it, because we have permitted it to do so. We supinely let the federal government right any wrong, regulate any behavior, tax any event, start any war, kill any foe, seize any property and crush any liberty as if our rights came from it, and as if the Constitution has no meaning or authority.

This is the same government that can't deliver the mail, fill potholes, stop robocalls, spend within its means, abide by the laws that it has written or follow the Constitution—and Biden wants it to force vaccinate us!

All modern presidents have misunderstood their obligations under the Constitution. From Wilson to Biden, they have argued that their first job is to keep us safe. That obligation is self-assumed. Their first job under the Constitution is to keep us free. Even if the government keeps us safe but unfree, we have the duty to alter or abolish it.

Chapter 22

Dr. Denis Rancourt and several fellow Canadian academics penned an open letter to support those who have decided not to accept the COVID-19 vaccine. Their names are penned in at the end of this chapter.

The group emphasizes the voluntary nature of this medical treatment as well as the need for informed consent and individual risk-benefit assessment. They reject the pressure exerted by public health officials, the news and social media, and fellow citizens.

Control over our bodily integrity may well be the ultimate frontier of the fight to protect civil liberties.

Open letter to the unvaccinated

You are not alone! As of July 28, 2021, 29% of Canadians have not received a COVID-19 vaccine, and an additional 14% have received one shot. In the U.S. and in the European Union, less than half the population is fully vaccinated, and even in Israel, the "world's lab" according to Pfizer, one third of people remain completely unvaccinated. Politicians and the media have taken a uniform view, scapegoating the unvaccinated for the troubles that have ensued after many months of fearmongering and lockdowns. It's time to set the record straight.

It is entirely reasonable and legitimate to say 'no' to insufficiently tested vaccines for which there is no reliable science.

You have a right to assert guardianship of your body and to refuse medical treatments if you see fit. You have a right to say 'no' to a violation of your dignity, your integrity and your bodily autonomy. It is your body, and you have a right to choose. You are right to fight for your children against their mass vaccination in school.

You are right to question whether free and informed consent is at all possible under present circumstances. Long-term effects are unknown. Transgenerational effects are unknown. Vaccine-induced deregulation of natural immunity is unknown. Potential harm is unknown as the adverse event reporting is delayed, incomplete and inconsistent between jurisdictions.

You are being targeted by mainstream media, government social engineering campaigns, unjust rules and policies, collaborating employers, and the social-media mob.

You are being told that you are now the problem and that the world cannot get back to normal unless you are vaccinated.

You're being scapegoated by propaganda and pressured by others around you. Remember, there is nothing wrong with you.

You are inaccurately accused of being a factory for new SARS-CoV-2 variants, when in fact, according to leading scientists, your natural immune system generates immunity to multiple components of the virus. This will promote your protection against a vast range of viral variants and abrogates further spreading to anyone else.

You are justified in demanding independent peer-reviewed studies, not funded by multinational pharmaceutical companies. All the peer-reviewed studies of short-term safety and short-term efficacy have been funded, organized, coordinated, and supported by these for-profit corporations and none of the study data have been made public or available to researchers who don't work for these companies.

PANDEMIC PANDEMONIUM

You are right to question the preliminary vaccine trial results. The claimed high values of relative efficacy rely on small numbers of tenuously determined "infections." The studies were also not all blind, where the people giving the injections admittedly knew or could deduce whether they were injecting the experimental vaccine or the placebo. This is not acceptable scientific methodology for vaccine trials.

You are correct in your calls for a diversity of scientific opinions. Like in nature, we need a polyculture of information and its interpretations. And we don't have that right now. Choosing not to take the vaccine is holding space for reason, transparency and accountability to emerge. You are right to ask, "What comes next when we give away authority over our own bodies?"

Do not be intimidated. You are showing resilience, integrity and grit. You are coming together in your communities, making plans to help one another and standing for scientific accountability and free speech, which are required for society to thrive. We are among many who stand with you.

Angela Durante, PhD, Denis Rancourt, PhD, Claus Rinner, PhD, Laurent Leduc, PhD, Donald Welsh, PhD, John Zwaagstra, PhD, Jan Vrbik, PhD, Valentina Capurri, PhD

Chapter 23

By Richard Gale & Gary Null, PhD

Gary Null, PhD is an internationally renowned expert in the field of health and nutrition and is the author of over 70 best-selling books on healthy living and the director of over 100 critically acclaimed full-feature documentary films on natural health, self-empowerment and the environment. He is the host of the "Gary Null Show," the country's longest running nationally syndicated health radio talk show. Throughout his career Gary Null has made hundreds of radio and television broadcasts throughout the country as an environmentalist, consumer advocate, investigative reporter and nutrition educator.

Have the artchitects of COVID-19 lost touch with reality?

As the pandemic wages on, two diametrically opposed movements have consolidated in defiance against each other. The dominant contingent, represented by Biden, Congress, Anthony Fauci, Bill Gates and the mainstream media, has decided that any citizen who refuses a COVID-19 vaccine is a de facto enemy of the state. Ultimately, Joe Biden declared during another gaffe remark about the status of the government's vaccination campaign, "those who are not vaccinated will pay—end up paying the price." Despite the dubious claims that the mRNA is approximately 95% effective, the unvaccinated therefore mysteriously pose a health risk to the vaccinated. Consequently, any punitive actions the federal and the state governments undertake, including encouraging the social media to publicly shame and censor voices of caution and reason, are justified.

In an effort to marginalize and socially victimize Israeli citizens who have postponed or refused vaccination, Netanyahu and his supporters passed a bill permitting personal information and data about unvaccinated citizens to be shared across government agencies and civil institutions. Israel was named by Pfizer's CEO as the "world's lab" for the company's COVID-19 rollout. Contrary to the government's response to criticisms, the unvaccinated are theoretically second-class citizens branded with a "scarlet letter" depriving them of full engagement with Israeli society, including going to a restaurant, attending a movie, concert or athletic event. Many are unable to shop or go to work. Even the staunch pro-Zionist New York Times indicated the government's policies are "moving in the direction of a two-tier system for the vaccinated and the unvaccinated."

A civilian organization, the Israeli People Committee, which includes many health professionals, released a devastating report on the number of injuries and deaths resulting from Pfizer's vaccine. It was during the peak of the government's vaccination campaign that Israel experienced its highest mortality rate, especially among those between 20 and 29 years of age. The Committee reported "26 percent of all cardiac events occurred in young people up to the age of 40, with the most common diagnosis in these cases being myositis and pericarditis." Other adverse vaccine reactions included infarction, stroke, miscarriage, impaired blood circulation and pulmonary embolisms.

Nevertheless, Israel has become the "poster child" for far more than serving as Pfizer's experimental laboratory for human ferrets. It also models a caste society of haves and have nots, the rewarded and the repressed, the vaccine-anointed and the untouchables, as strategized by the World Economic Forum's future technological proposals in its Great Reset.

Last October, during the WEF's "Great Reset" virtual session, Netanyahu appeared with Columbia's far-right president Ivan Dugue—polled as the least popular president during the nation's history -- and Rwanda's war criminal Paul Kagame, along with executives in the biotech and financial industries, to advocate on behalf of the Forum's mantra that the pandemic is an "opportunity" to further mobilize global digital infrastructure systems, including COVID-19 vaccination verification via microchip technology.

Now we are witnessing Canada, the U.K. and the U.S. aggressively mimicking Israel's heavy-handed policies to establish full-spectrum social control and make efforts to implement a post-modern, technologically driven caste system. Although Biden stated he does not support a federal mandate on vaccination passports, it has been left to the individual states to decide. Democrat-controlled states, notably New York, are issuing vaccine passports as a ticket to return to normal. Republican governors on the other hand have been quick to denounce them, and in the case of Arizona, Florida, Idaho, Montana, and Texas to executively ban them altogether. Hopefully some of the bans will challenge many of the over 100 private colleges and universities that decided to require students to be vaccinated before returning in the Fall.

The mainstream corporate media spews volleys of baseless news that the vaccines are effective and wholly safe. However, thousands of medical school professors, physicians and researchers are challenging this non-consensual assumption. They regularly point out that there is no reliable science to justify any such claims. This raises the question: what are the vaccines effective against? Surely not contracting SARS-CoV-2; thousands of fully vaccinated people are testing positive with the infection. The CDC reported "seven percent of those vaccinated who have been infected have been hospitalized and 74 have died."

Government efforts to reach a fictitious herd immunity threshold will inevitably come at a great cost to human life.

More recent studies suggest that an exceedingly large percentage of Americans should technically be exempt from COVID-19 vaccines. The University of Michigan published a recent analysis suggesting that three percent of vaccinated Americans taking immune-weakening drugs have an increased risk of hospitalization. The study is grossly conservative and undermines the breadth of the problem. The researchers only analyzed patients with private insurance, under the age of 65, and who were only prescribed immunosuppressive steroids, such as corticosteroids and prednisone. Other immunosuppressive drugs were seemingly excluded from the Michigan analysis. Thirty-three percent of the American population was therefore excluded from the study because, according to the CDC, only 66.8 percent of the population has private health insurance. New York University researchers reported in a British medical journal that a third of patients receiving methotrexate and TNF inhibitors for immune-medicated inflammatory illnesses such as rheumatoid arthritis and psoriasis fail to achieve sufficient antibodies from the Pfizer vaccine. We are certain that this will be found equally true for many other medications if or when studies are conducted.

Consequently, a very conservative 17 percent of Americans are at greater risk from either viral infection or vaccine injury death. This also excludes tens of millions of adults (30 percent) and children (40 percent) with chronic allergies and many of the over 89,000 cancer patients diagnosed annually and prescribed chemotherapeutic drugs. Every year, nearly two-thirds of all Americans require emergency medical care from allergic reactions alone. Furthermore, those with certain immune weaknesses are less likely to generate sufficient vaccine-induced antibodies thereby making COVID-19 vaccination ineffective.

Especially disturbing is that the clinical trials the FDA relied upon for Emergency Use Authorization for the past five months of the vaccination campaign were based upon enrollment of healthy participants. Only recently are clinical trials either underway or in recruitment to test the vaccines on participants with weakened immune systems, including small children and infants, and on pregnant women. In the meantime, millions of immunosuppressed people diagnosed with autoimmune conditions or pre-existing comorbidities, from young to old, are being indiscriminately injected. This has been a policy enacted so far on the elderly, the sickly, the immune-compromised, pregnant moms, and the rest of the nation. It is not irrational, therefore, to suspect that past and present COVID-19 trials have been conducted with malice of forethought and with the unconditional approval of our federal health officials.

During the pandemic, the rapid ascent of our vaccine-addicted culture's mantra of "vaccination at any cost" truly borders on medical malfeasance and criminal negligence. The overriding emphasis on vaccination and near total disregard for implementing very simple preventative measures to inhibit infections from progressing in severity. If our health policy-makers were wise men and women, alternative treatments such as ivermectin, hydroxychloroquine, and more recent inexpensive off-patent drugs, which have been shown to be highly effective for early stage treatment and being widely prescribed elsewhere in the world, would be permitted and encouraged without reservation. There would be no reason to wait for a novel drug costing thousands of dollars per patient to arrive. And we still await that magic bullet drug because the previous one, remdesivir, was a faulty blank. This is just another example of the institutionalized pathology that infects our health agencies.

There is no convincing science to support our federal officials' belief that a previously infected person requires a COVID-19 vaccine to acquire immunity. In fact, more recent research indicates the opposite and goes directly against the intellectually fetid arguments of the financier Bill Gates that every person on the planet should be vaccinated without exception. Johns Hopkins University professor Dr. Marty Makary has put forth the evidence that "natural immunity works." Makary notes that it is only the rare instance when a person is being re-infected. Washington University School of Medicine reported this month that even mild COVID-19 infections induce long lasting antibody protection. The study's lead researcher Dr. Ali Ellebedy stated. . .

"Last fall, there were reports that antibodies wane quickly after infection with the virus that causes COVID-19, and mainstream media interpreted that to mean that immunity was not long-lived. . . But that's a misinterpretation of the data. It's normal for antibody levels to go down after acute infection, but they don't go down to zero; they plateau. Here, we found antibody-producing cells in people 11 months after the first symptoms. These cells live and produce antibodies for the rest of people's lives. That's strong evidence for long-lasting immunity."

The information we were fed to downplay natural immunity was wrong at best, and more likely a lie, in order to further persuade the public into the importance of the vaccines to return their lives to normal. Another study appearing in this month's Journal of Infectious Diseases found that "SARS-CoV-2 specific immune memory response [following infection] persists in most patients nearly one year after infection." The COVID-19 vaccines can't make the same promise. In fact, more reports show that fully vaccinated persons are becoming infected. But it gets worse...

The pro-vaccine argument wrongly assumes that anyone who refuses the COVID-19 is therefore an anti-vaxxer. We would argue it is rational caution in the face of a national healthcare system indebted to the pharmaceutical industry and that is rapidly losing public trust. Likewise, if a doctor is successfully treating hundreds of patients without a reported death with cheap, effective drugs, he or she is cancelled and ridiculed as a quack. Instead of open dialogue and debate, those who challenge this are censored from all social platforms. This is despite the impeccable credentials of many medical professionals abiding by the precautionary principle and who dare to challenge Anthony Fauci and Bill Gates, whose faux philanthropy is nothing less than a profitmaking enterprise like Microsoft.

Conflicts of interest, both financial and non-financial, are endemic in our medical system. Therefore, it becomes increasingly more difficult to trust any clinical study or government policy that is based upon flawed evidence submitted by a drug maker that fails to undergo a thorough independent and impartial review by qualified medical experts. There is a clear psychological reason for this. Many psychologists have pointed out over the years that "cognitive bias," "motivated reasoning" driving the evaluation of clinical trial data and the subsequent institutional regulatory review and decision-making are deeply contrary and undermine the entire evidence-based criteria that should oversee what drugs, vaccines, medical devices, therapeutic protocols should be recommended or approved for use upon the public.

The late Scott Lilienfeld, a professor of psychology at Emory University, writes, "Clinicians are subject to the same errors in thinking that affect virtually all people. In particular, practitioners must be wary of (a) the misuse of certain heuristics (e.g., availability, representativeness) and (b) cognitive biases (e.g., confirmation bias) in their everyday work." Although Lilienfeld is singling out clinical physicians, it applies more rigorously and accurately to the pharmaceutical presidents, CEOs and chief science officers overseeing vaccine development who have stock prices to reach and shareholders to please. Cognitive bias equally plagues the entire executive hierarchy at the CDC, NIAID, FDA and HHS who are beholden to the gaping revolving door between these agencies and private industry and their revenues. Writing about the deep ethical concerns behind bias in our medical institutions. Dr Thomas Murray, president of the Hastings Center, states, "For scientists on a panel of the Food and Drug Administration, for example, it isn't immediately clear to whom they owe their primary loyalty." Such biases, Murray believes, have completely destroyed the credibility of the World Health Organization.

The fact that rates to reproduce medical clinical trials are so poor, according to one esteemed behavioral economist, is that "cognitive biases may be the reason for that." It also explains why Stanford University Medical School professor John Ioannidis argues, "most published research findings false, and an 85 percent of research resources are wasted." Junk science based upon bias should also include every vaccine application submitted to the FDA for regulatory approval, since the vaccine companies are privileged to cherry-pick whichever trials they want to submit to create the most promising portfolio.

One could review all of the official decisions made during the past 17 months—by Anthony Fauci, Trump and Biden and the naive stances in both political parties—and should easily observe the frailties of cognitive bias and repeated contradictions throughout. None whatsoever are reliably truthful. And of course, cognitive bias leads to cognitive dissonance, such as denying that one has a bias or resorting to flagrant rejection and disparagement in order to avoid any scientific data that conflicts with one's unfounded beliefs.

We now live in a nation with bureaucratic decree rather than by immunological science. This is postmodern cultism at its worst because it hides behind the veneer of being scientific. And it has the full support of a political technocracy that can ordain authoritarian laws. There is a dire need for a collective epiphany. All of us are experiencing the pandemic as a failed experiment orchestrated by institutions that have lost touch with reality. And it has been a very deadly experiment due to the extraordinary incompetence of our medical-degreed bureaucrats. Sadly, the decades of institutional ineptitude have had to reach national and perhaps global awareness at this time when the powers that possess every technological tool at their disposal to conduct wide surveillance, pass undemocratic and draconian laws with full impunity, and control the fenced sheep within the mainstream media.

Chapter 24

The Prevailing Corona Nonsense Narrative

By Dr. Thomas Binder—Dec. 25, 2021

I studied medicine at the University of Zurich, obtained a doctorate in immunology and virology, specialized in internal medicine and cardiology and have 33 years of experience in diagnosis and therapy of acute respiratory infections, in hospitals in intensive care units and, for 23 years, in my medical practice.

In February 2020, I sat in my practice and was amazed. What I had learned in medical school, during my scientific training and in my practical medical work was suddenly turned upside down. Anyone who felt even a sore throat, no longer treated himself, but ran to the nearest hospital with the request to be tested immediately, and with the fear of perhaps having to die; not only having to die, but perhaps having to suffocate miserably.

Worldwide, the prevailing corona narrative was established in a very short period. At the same time, humanity was divided into its supporters and opponents.

Such an extent of division of the society we have never experienced before. It divides friendships, families, and even partnerships. Such a division is always an expression of the fact that a large part of humanity is not living in reality, but is caught up in a context of delusion imposed by a handful of psychopaths and their narcissistic lackeys. In such a situation we must always ask ourselves first: "Am I a realist, or in fact a totally deluded one?" This question can only be answered by looking at reality as soberly as possible.

It is my duty as a doctor to treat my patients to the best of my knowledge. This includes to inform them about their disease in a way that laypeople can understand and make informed decisions about what to do.

In February/March 2020 I realized that it is my duty as a doctor to educate the public about this disease of the whole society, in a way that laypeople can understand and make informed decisions about what to do. I am still doing this, no more but also no less, and nobody and nothing will stop me from continuing to do so.

I confront the myths and intellectual absurdities of the prevailing corona narrative with the scientific evidence. I do this chronologically and so that also laypeople can understand and also make informed decisions as to what further actions seem appropriate, for themselves and for their loved ones.

Scientific references to my statements can be found on homepages of 'Aletheia—our Swiss network of doctors and scientists for proportionality' of the 'Corman-Droston Review Report' and of 'Doctors for COVID Ethics', all of which I am a member, and on my simple homepage, which I had created after having been banned from social media.

PCR testing epidemic, 2006

As responsible physicians and scientists, in the case of infections diagnosed by quick PCR tests, especially in the context of an alleged epidemic of national or pandemic of international scope, we must always consider the possibility of a pseudo or testing epidemic.

In 2007, the New York Times, virtually the bible of journalists whose integrity they still trusted at the time, publishes an important piece entitled: 'Faith in Quick Test Leads to Epidemic That Wasn't'.

A leading internist at a medical center in the U.S. state of New Hampshire, coughs seemingly incessantly for a fortnight starting in mid-April 2006. Soon, an infectious disease specialist has the disturbing idea that this could be the beginning of a pertussis epidemic. By the end of April, other hospital staff are also coughing. Severe, persistent coughing is a leading symptom of whooping cough. And if it is whooping cough, the outbreak must be contained immediately because the disease can be fatal for babies in the hospital and lead to dangerous pneumonia in frail elderly patients.

It is the start of a bizarre episode: the story of an epidemic that wasn't.

For months, almost everyone involved believes there is a huge whooping cough outbreak at the medical center with far-reaching consequences. Nearly 1,000 staff members are given a quick PCR test and put on leave from work until the results are in; 142 people, 14.2% of those tested are positive on the quick PCR test and diagnosed with pertussis. Thousands including many children, receive antibiotics and a vaccine as protection. Hospital beds are taken out of service as a precaution, including some in the intensive care unit.

Months later, all those apparently suffering from whopping cough are stunned to learn that bacterial cultures, the diagnosis gold standard for pertussis, could not detect the bacterium that causes whopping cough in any single sample. This whole insanity was a false alarm.

The supposed pertussis epidemic had not taken place in reality, but only in the minds of those involved, triggered by blind faith in a highly sensitive quick PCR test had had become oh, so modern. In truth, all those who had fallen ill had suffered from a harmless cold. Infectiologists and epidemiologists had put aside their expertise and common sense and blatantly ignored this most likely differential diagnosis of the symptom cough.

Many of the new molecular tests are quick but technically demanding. Each laboratory performs them in their own way as so-called 'home brews.' Often, they are not commercially available and there are rarely good estimates of their error rates. Their high sensitivity makes false positives likely. When hundreds or thousands of people are tested, as happened here, false-positive results can give the appearance of an epidemic.

As an infectiologist said, "I had the feeling at the same time that this gave us a shadow of a hint of what it might be like during a pandemic flu epidemic."

An epidemiologist explained: One of the most troubling aspects of the pseudo-epidemic is that all the decisions seemed so sensible at the time.

'Event 201: Corona Pandemic Simulation, 2019'
(As seen on Google)

The situation is threatening. A new corona virus is spreading across the world. Case numbers on the Johns Hopkins University dashboard are rising and rising. The highly contagious, immune-resistant, dangerous virus is paralyzing trade and transport globally and sending the world economy into free-fall.

What sounds like the alleged outbreak of the alleged pandemic of Sars-CoV-2 in China's Wuhan province in December 2019, is the scenario of 'Event 201, 'which because the figure zero is actually a globe, should rather be called 'Event 21.'

On October 18, 2019, Bill and Melinda Gates Foundation, Johns Hopkins University and World Economic Forum are organizing a pandemic simulation under this name. After the Spanish flu, the bird flu, and the swine flu, they do not choose another influenza virus as pathogen, but a corona virus that was completely unknown to the laypeople so far, especially not to politicians and journalists.

The simulation of a corona pandemic that broke out in South America is not attended by doctors, but by Western representatives of the organizers, the UN, the WHO governments, authorities and global corporations from the fields of high finance, pharmaceuticals, logistics, tourism and the media, as well as George Gao, virologist and director of the Chinese Center for Disease Control and Prevention (CDC).

The Event 201 Pandemic Exercise, October 18, 2019 also addressed within the simulation how to deal with online social media and so-called "misinformation."

The participants agree that a corona pandemic is disruptive, can only be overcome by global governmental and private cooperation, that system-relevant global corporations must be propped up financially while medium-sized businesses must be sacrificed if necessary, that voices who deviate from the prevailing narrative must be censored consistently in the social and mass media, and that the pandemic can only be terminated by vaccinating the entire world population.

The entities directly or indirectly "represented" by the "players" included the WHO, Johns Hopkins, the Global Alliance on Vaccines and Immunization (GAVI) (Dr. Thomas Grant Evans), the U.S. Intelligence, the Bill and Melinda Gates Foundation (Dr. Chris Elias), the Coalition for Epidemic Preparedness Innovations (CEPI) (Chairwoman Jane Halton), the World Economic Forum (WEF) the UN Foundation, the U.S. Centers for Disease Control and Prevention (CDC) (Director Dr. George Fu Gao), Big Pharma (Adrian Thomas), the World Bank and Global Banking, the Airline and Hotel Industries.

The simulation ends with 65 million deaths worldwide.

I recommend you watch the documentary 'Event 201: Corona Pandemic from the Drafting Table,' produced in German with English subtitles by ExpressZeitung in June 2020, and ask yourself: Shouldn't the mass media have reported this in detail?

Corona scandal, 2020 and ongoing

Two-and-a-half months later, on December 31, 2019, the Chinese CDC, led by Dr. George Gao Fu, reports 27 cases of pneumonia of unknown cause to the WHO—out of a Chinese population of 1.4 billion. On January 7th 2020, the Chinese health authorities identify a novel corona virus as the causative agent.

On January 21st, Prof. Christian Drosten et al. submits a paper, the recipe for which laboratories can produce a rapid RT-PCR test for detection of the virus called '2019-nCoV.' It is accepted just the next day and published in the Journal Eurosurveillance another day later.

The WHO had already posted the Corman-Drosten RT-PCR quick test on its website one week earlier are recommended it as the global diagnostic gold standard.

On January 30th, Drosten et al. published the justification of the narrative of epidemiologically relevant asymptomatic transmission of 2019-nCoV in the letter to the editor of the 'New England Journal of Medicine,' virtually one of the bibles of us doctors whose integrity we still trusted at the time, with the title, 'Transmission of 2019-nCoV Infection From an Asymptomatic Contact in Germany.'

On February 11th the WHO names the novel corona virus SARS-CoV-2, the disease it causes COVID-19; coronavirus disease. It does so against the request of Chinese virologists. They preferred to call it HCoV-19, human coronavirus, because the danger that the name SARS-COV-2 could stir up with unfounded fears out of its biological and epidemiological lack of similarity to the much more dangerous SARS-CoV-1.

On March 11th, the WHO declares a COVID pandemic. Meanwhile, its Director-General, the biologist, immunologist and philosopher Dr. Tedros Ghebreyesus, has been charged with genocide in Ethiopia before the International Criminal Court in Hague. The presumption of innocence applies, of course.

Now, almost everything is going on as it did during the swine flu scandal in 2009, but in an even more lubricated way. Experts, mostly laboratory physicians and biologists working as virologists or epidemiologists, who have never examined anyone suffering from a respiratory infection, let alone treated them, declare that SARS-CoV-2 is virtually an alien about which we know absolutely nothing and that we must regard as extremely dangerous, until largely, the same experts will have proven otherwise at some point. In Switzerland, they constitute themselves as 'Swiss National COVID-19 Science Task Force' and offer themselves to the Swiss Federal Council as scientific advisors.

The executive and legislative politicians as well as the federal and cantonal health authorities, all panicked by them, accept their offer and seem to follow them as blindly as the Federal Council apparently blindly followed the WHO when it declared the COVID pandemic. Unlike any ninepins club, the now official scientific advisory board to the Swiss government through what is supposed to be Switzerland's biggest crisis since the Second World War does not keep any record of its activities.

On March 16th, the Swiss Federal Council declares the 'exceptional situation,' the highest danger level of the epidemic law, based on exactly zero scientific evidence.

The mass media, including the Swiss public service broadcaster SRG, take on the third part in this conglomerate of mutually escalating ignorance, arrogance, incompetence and organized irresponsibility. Brainless and heartless themselves, they hammer into our heads around the clock:

There is a pandemic of a highly contagious and even epidemiologically relevant asymptomatically transmissible corona killer virus. Every seemingly hale and hearty fellow human being can be your angel of death!

Unlike in 2009, the mass media consistently censor, discredit and defame questioning doctors and scientists, including luminaries such as John Ioannidis, Professor of medicine, epidemiology and public health at Stanford University School of Medicine. He is one of the world's most renowned and most cited scientists, who specialized in science fraud.

The governments of almost all countries seem to have forgotten their epidemic plans which wisely spare the individuals, the society and the economy. In blind obedience to the WHO and to lobbyists, called experts, they are enacting self-destructive non-pharmacological interventions, including lockdowns never considered before, following the authoritarian Chinese role model. They are doing this almost globally, in lockstep.

Without consulting the population, they procure billions of doses of emergency mRNA and DNA injections which are even temporarily approved by Swissmedic. This technology is being widely used on humans for the first time. Almost worldwide, the constitution, the rule of law, human rights, civil liberties, ethics, science and common sense are being sacrificed in favor of a quasi-global authoritarian regime under the control of the WHO.

Who controls the WHO, controls the world!

The prevailing corona narrative is this: Since early 2020, there is a pandemic of a perennial killer virus, that must be searched for with the Corman-Drosten PT-PTR test in everybody, that is even spreading epidemiologically relevantly asymptomatically, against which there is no basic or cross-immunity, whose provoked disease, COVID-19 is barely treatable, which is becoming increasingly infectious and dangerous due to erratic mutations, and which can only be overcome by non-pharmacological measures that have never been applied before, such as antisocial distancing, masks in public sphere, contact tracing, isolation, quarantine, school closures and curfews, nowadays called lockdowns, even for asymptomatic, previously called healthy people, and by serial vaccination of the entire world population.

In many countries, for example, in Switzerland, there was no exceptional excess mortality when adjusted to changing the demographics. The excess mortality in other countries is the best proof that the real killer is not the virus, but our paradoxical response to it, which differs from country to country and from jurisdiction to jurisdiction. Also, the occupancy of the intensive care units, whose capacities have been massively reduced in the course of the alleged pandemic, has never been unusually high.

Chapter 25

Vaccine mandate protests go global

I saw a news report on One America News (OAN) showing an image of thousands of people gathered in Piazza del Popolo square, during a protest in Rome, Saturday, October 9, 2021. Prominently shown, was this massive crowd holding up a large sign which read "Asciano—No Green Pass." Underneath was stated: "People gather in Piazza del Popolo square during a protest in Rome, Saturday, October 9, 2021. Thousands of demonstrators protested Saturday in Rome against the COVID-19 health pass that Italian workers in both the public and private sectors must display to access their workplaces from Oct. 15, under a government decree."

OAN Newsroom—October 11, 2021

Police clashed with protesters in Rome after an anti-forced vaccination protest descended into violence. Italy has planned to introduce its "Green Pass" in a week, which prompted thousands of Italians to take to the streets to protest the government on Saturday.

The Green Pass would be among the strictest vaccine requirements in the world. Italians who do not have proof of vaccination, previous infection or a negative test will not be allowed to enter work to make a living.

PANDEMIC PANDEMONIUM

The crowd of protesters became frenzied when police tried to stop them from marching down the street. Water cannons were fired at citizens and numerous others were arrested.

Italy was not alone in citizens being irate at their government for forcing vaccinations. Neighboring Slovenia saw thousands of people descend on the capital from all across the country to protest restrictions and mandates.

While not as strict as Italy, all Slovenians have been forced to either prove a vaccine or negative test at personal expense to attend work at state run firms. The protest coincided with a European Union summit taking place in the Capital, which prompted police to stop 30 buses from entering the city with protesters from other parts of the country.

Helicopters were closely monitoring the event, but police still launched tear gas and water cannons at citizens as they tried to march through the city. Protesters demanded an end to "corona fascism" in their country, which has the lowest vaccination rate across Europe at 48%.

Europe is not exclusive with protests against mandates. In New York City, the most populated in the United States, there have been protests against the pass as well.

The protests have drawn thousands of people in attendance. New Yorkers have been calling on the government for the freedom to choose whether to receive the vaccine or not.

In New York, Mayor Bill de Blasio has pushed through the most extensive mandate for vaccines in the U.S. He has required people to show proof of vaccination to enter restaurants, bars and theaters. There are no exemptions for those with natural immunity or those with religious objections to taking the jab.

On top of the city mandate, a statewide mandate has forced all health care and nursing home workers to take the shot or be fired. This has exacerbated an already existing shortage of workers in the field.

The protests taking place all across the world have the general goal which is freedom for citizens to make medical decisions for themselves, without being cast out from making a living.

I captured a video and recording which was shown on OAN (One America News) of an airline pilot who was not mentioned by name, but the video went viral and was captioned as follows:

Man claiming to be airline pilot releases impassioned video, says vaccine & other mandates are stripping away freedom to choose

As pilots for major airlines protest vaccine mandates, a man who claims to be an airline pilot released a passionate video that has gone viral.

"I've been an airline pilot for 18 years, and now I've been given an ultimatum. Not a choice, but an ultimatum. I've been told in order to continue my career as an airline pilot I must be vaccinated, which really means I have to choose between putting food on the table for my family and my freedom of choice. Whether you believe vaccination is the right thing to do or not, the situation goes far beyond health, with the American people having fought for freedom for 257 years. We go around the world spreading ideas of freedom and democracy. We help other counties and people fight for their freedoms while ours are being stripped away. You may think being forced to wear a mask or getting a vaccination is insignificant. But when you begin to compile mandate after mandate and loss of freedom after freedom it becomes very significant. As each thing is taken away, we face what is known as the shifting baseline syndrome. This syndrome changes our idea of what is normal and what is not normal. Soon we will not remember what it was like to have the freedoms we once did. Our children and our grandchildren will experience less freedom and they won't have the privilege or the pleasure to enjoy the same choices our parents had or that we have. If we give into these mandates, we dishonor every service person over the last 257 years; a disservice to the people who fought and bled for the very freedoms we enjoy. Whether you believe in vaccination or not, I'm standing up for your freedom of choice. You may support the vaccine mandates because they are in line with your current beliefs. But if we let this happen now there will be a day when what you're told to do will not fall in line with your beliefs. If we do not stand together and fight back with one voice, soon we could be told where to live, what job we will do, what religion to believe and how many children we can have. Do you really want someone telling your children or your grandchildren what, when, and how they will live every minute of their lives? It's time we take a stance; it's time we fight for our freedom of choice while we still can. Join us!"

Chapter 26

Forced vaccination was always the end game. American's move towards

By Barbara Loe Fisher, co-founder and president of the National Vaccine Information Center (NVIC)

The NVIC is a non-profit charity she founded with parents of vaccine injured children in 1982 to prevent vaccine injuries and deaths through public education. For the past four decades, she has led a national, grassroots movement and public information campaign to institute vaccine safety and informed consent protections in public health policies and laws. She has researched, analyzed and publicly articulated the science, policy, law, ethics and politics of vaccination to become one of the world's leading non-medical, consumer advocacy experts on vaccination and human rights. She says as follows:

With the exception of Pearl Harbor and September 11, 2001, Americans have not been attacked by an enemy on our own soil. Unlike countries in Europe during World War II, America has never been occupied by a military force or locked down under martial law.

We have never seen soldiers in armored vehicles patrolling the streets, warning us to stay in our homes or face arrest—or worse.

PANDEMIC PANDEMONIUM

Beginning in 1776, when our freedom seeking founders wrote the Declaration of Independence and stood their ground from Lexington and Concord to Saratoga and Valley Forge, and then came together to create a constitutional Republic dedicated to protecting individual and minority rights, the United States of America has defined and served as a beacon of liberty for people around the world.

This summer we watched soldiers patrolling the streets of Sydney, Australia with helicopters overhead blaring warnings to a stunned, locked down people to stay in their homes in the name of public health.

We have watched hundreds of thousands of people, young and old, gather together again and again in the streets of Paris, London, Rome, Athens, and Berlin. They are marching against authoritarianism embodied in government issued vaccine passports that punish citizens for simply defending the right to make a voluntary medical decision for themselves and their minor children, a decision about whether to be injected with a biological pharmaceutical product that can cause serious reactions, injure, kill, or fail to work.

The signs they carry say:

"No Forced Testing, no force vaccines"

"Stop the dictatorship"

"Hands off our children"

"My body is mine"

"Big Pharma shackles freedom"

"No to the Pass of shame"

"Better to die free than live as a slave"

In what has become a prophetic primal scream for liberty, governments are ordering the police to break up the largely peaceful demonstrators flooding the big cities and small villages of western Europe, the first populations to organize massive public protests against old fashioned tyranny dressed up in 21st century clothes.

The people of Europe were the first to stand up for freedom during this government declared public health emergency because they know how tyranny begins. They know what it looks like and they remember what it feels like. They remember and are declaring, "Never again."

In America, we have taken our freedom for granted

Most Americans today do not remember World War II, or if they do, it is what their parents or grandparents told them about it. World War II was not fought on American soil. Americans went to war in Europe to stop the slaughter of millions at the hands of an authoritarian fascist government commanding the Army of the Third Reich that killed in the name of public health and safety and even an authoritarian communist government slaughtered many more millions during a "Reign of Terror" in the Soviet Union. Most American children today are not taught what happened in China after World War II, when the Chinese Communist Party (CCP) implemented the Great Leap Forward and the Great Proletarian Cultural Revolution. Those militant ideological cleansing campaigns imprisoned and killed tens of millions of citizens because they criticized or opposed authoritarian government policies.

In America we have taken our freedom for granted because, while we are willing to fight to defend the freedom of others, we have never been called on to defend it in our own backyard. Most Americans have never imagined we would experience a serious threat to autonomy and freedom of thought, speech, conscience and assembly. So deep has been our trust in the laws and cultural values, which have for the most part ensured fundamental freedoms in our country that we never believed it could happen here.

But the last 20 months have changed everything. Many Americans have begun to understand that tyranny can be disguised to look like safety, even as many others cannot bring themselves to believe it.

American's move toward authoritarianism

Striking fear into the hearts and minds of people, the move towards authoritarianism in America began with government officials suddenly telling us—even children as young as two years old—that we could not breathe fresh air or enter public spaces without a mask covering our face. Millions of American workers judged to be "non-essential" lost the ability to earn a living so they could eat and pay rent. During "flatten the curve" lockdowns we were told it would only last a few weeks but, instead, went on for months. Anyone who criticized government narratives about the origin of SARS-CoV-2 virus or questioned social distancing restrictions was immediately publicly shamed and censored. Any doctor, who tried to prove early treatment to COVID-19 patients by repurposing safe and effective licensed drugs and nutritional supplements to help their patients survive the infection, were also publicly shamed and censored.

After the FDA granted Pfizer and Moderna an Emergency Use Authorization (EUA) in December 2020 to distribute their liability free experimental mRNA COVID-19 vaccines in the U.S., public health officials enlisted big corporations to launch a hard-sell national vaccine advertising campaign targeting all Americans over the age of 12. Anyone who asked questions or challenged the hard sell was immediately censored on social media. State governments and employers were encouraged to threaten workers, especially health care workers and emergency responders, with loss of their jobs for refusing the vaccine. Private businesses were encouraged to deny unvaccinated citizens entry to restaurants, stores, and other public venues.

By the end of July 2021, the Department of Veteran Affairs directed all VA health care workers to be fully vaccinated or lose their jobs. In early August, the Department of Defense announced at all Military Service members must be fully vaccinated when the FDA officially licenses a COVID-19 vaccine or lose their jobs. Suddenly, on Aug. 23, the Pfizer mRNA vaccine was licensed without a public meeting of the FDA Vaccines and Related Biological Products Advisory Committee (VRPBAC) and full disclosure of the scientific data supporting licensure.

By the end of August, about 176 million Americans had been "fully vaccinated, representing 53.6 percent of our population of 333 million people, which was the third largest in the world. And studies had confirmed that the SARS-CoV-2 infection mortality ratio (IFR) in the U.S. remains at less than one percent.

Federal government declares war on unvaccinated americans

The Executive Branch of the U.S. government was not happy. Federal health officials had publicly set the goal of persuading 90% of Americans to get the COVID vaccine, although it is clear now that the real goal all along was a 100% vaccination rate: no exceptions and no questions asked. The politics of persuasion gave way to an iron fisted approach using the heel of the boot of the State to try to club 100 million unvaccinated Americans into submission.

On Sept. 9, 2021, the President of the United States followed the advice of top public health officials and, in effect, declared war on unvaccinated Americans. He scapegoated and placed all the blame for the ongoing COVID-19 pandemic on the unvaccinated, even though federal health officials admit that fully vaccinated people can still get infected and transmit the virus to others, and even though breakthrough COVID infections, hospitalizations and deaths in fully vaccinated people are on the rise; and even though evidence shows individuals who have recovered from the infection have stronger natural immunity than those who have been vaccinated, and even though officials of the World Health Organization now say that the SARS-COV-2 virus is mutating like influenza and is likely to become prevalent in every country—no matter how high the vaccination rate.

The President told 100 million unvaccinated Americans that "our patience is running thin" and issued an Executive Order that every person working for the Executive Branch of the federal government—more than two million people—must get fully vaccinated or lose their jobs. That order also applied to about 17 million health care professionals working in medical facilities that accept Medicare and Medicaid.

There is no option for Executive Branch employees to get tested—the rule is get vaccinated or be fired. It is interesting that the order does not apply to workers in the Judicial Branch or Legislative Branch, which includes members and staffers in Congress.

The President also ordered the Department of Labor to issue a rule that carries penalties of $14,000 per violation to force private companies with more than 100 employees to get their workers fully vaccinated or be tested weekly. He also called for all teachers and school staff in all schools to be fully vaccinated.

The next day, the Director of the National Institute of Allergy and Infectious Diseases, Dr. Anthony Fauci, criticized the President for not going far enough. Fauci said the government should give Americans no option but to get injected with the biological product that some describe as a vaccine, others characterize as a genetic therapy or cell disrupter biological, and others allege it is a bioweapon made in a lab in China with U.S. funding. Then Fauci said all children must be vaccinated or denied a school education and all unvaccinated people must be banned from getting on an airplane. At the same time, a Virginia congressman introduced the Safety Travel Act that would require travelers getting on a plane or Amtrak train in the U.S. to show proof of COVID vaccination or a negative COVID test within 72 hours of boarding.

MYRNA SKOLLER
Destorying the lives of those who dissent

Today, people in some cities are being denied entrance to restaurants and stores if they can't prove they have been "fully" vaccinated. Doctors are refusing to provide medical care to the unvaccinated. Hollywood entertainers are celebrating the deaths of unvaccinated people, saying they deserved to die, and are calling for the unvaccinated who get COVID to be denied admission to hospitals for treatment. Judges are separating children from mothers who have not gotten a COVID shot.

Dissenters are told they are selfish and characterized as an enemy of the state for simply defending the human right to informed consent to medical risk taking. The normalizing of the ritualistic persecution of Americans who are refusing to give up the right to autonomy—which is a first and fundamental human right—is underway.

Demanding obedience, government health officials characterize public health policies that segregate, discriminate, and turn people against each other as "the good." Yet a lot of Americans instinctively know segregation and discrimination is not good. They know that persuading a majority of citizens to scapegoat a minority of citizens to cover up the failures of government is allowing evil to triumph.

Dissenting Americans, both vaccinated and unvaccinated, fill the ranks of every socio-economic class, every political party and every faith-based community. To understand the meaning of the warning that, "The only thing necessary for triumph of evil is for good men to do nothing," and they are not going to stand by and do nothing.

When government threatens to take away an individual's right to employment, education, health care and the ability to enter a store to buy food, enter a hospital or travel on public transportation, there is no other word for it but tyranny.

PANDEMIC PANDEMONIUM

Weaponizing a virus and a vaccine against the people

The virus, which has a 99% survival rate, and this leaky vaccine, which fails to reliably prevent infection and transmission in the fully vaccinated has racked up a record breaking more than half a million vaccine adverse event reports in the U.S. alone. It will not be the last virus and vaccine to be weaponized against the people in the name of greater good.

That is because forced vaccination is the tip of the spear in a culture war that has been going on for much longer than 40 years that I have been a vaccine safety and human rights activist publicly warning that this day would come. It is a war that will cause more suffering until enough of us refuse to be silenced, and instead, join together to change dangerous laws that abuse the trust and good will of the people.

Every single American, whether you have been vaccinated or not, should stop to reflect upon what is happening in our country. Think about what liberty means.

Imagine what life would be like in the future

Imagine what life will be like in the future if you cannot leave your home without being harnessed to a government issued digital ID, which contains personal information about your body and your life, and is hooked up to an electronic surveillance system that records and controls every move you make.

Imagine if you are a health care worker and your medical license is taken from you for refusing to get a government mandated vaccine, which is a public health policy being implemented in Washington, D.C., a city where doctors could vaccinate children as young as 11 years old without knowledge or consent of their parents.

Imagine if you cannot hold any type of job or enter a grocery store to buy food or feed your family, drug store, cafe, gym, school, cinema, museum, park, or beach without showing proof you've been vaccinated.

Imagine if you are denied entrance to a doctor's office or lose your Medicare and social security benefits because you don't have the vaccine passport, a suggestion made recently on national television.

Imagine if you cannot get on a plane or bus to visit your children or elderly parents because federal government officials have exercised authority over inter-state commerce and banned the unvaccinated from crossing state borders, an action that some proponents of forced vaccination are urging the current administration to invoke.

Imagine if you or your child have already suffered a previous serious vaccine reaction or have an underlying inflammatory immune disorder that increases your risk for being harmed by vaccination, but doctors refuse to see you because you are unvaccinated — which is already happening in America — and you are denied admission to a hospital for a lifesaving operation.

Forced vaccination was always the end game before and during this pandemic

If you think that the vaccine passport is only about this virus and this vaccine, think again. Forced vaccination was always the end game both before and during this pandemic and the proof of that lies in the decades of federal legislation and federal agency rule-making paving the way for what we are experiencing today. Right now, forced vaccination is the quickest means to what the World Economic Forum transparently describes on its website as "The Great Reset." You, your children and grandchildren are the commodity, and in the name of the greater good, you are expected to obediently allow others to "reset" your lives in all kinds of ways without making a sound.

The government issued passport allowing you to function in society, is just the first step on the slippery slope to what will be many more requirements and restrictions on your freedom in the days, months and years to come. The question is, will you allow yourself to be used and abused by those currently holding the power to do what they want to do to you, or will you defend your God-given right to life, liberty and the pursuit of happiness?

We can choose to live in fear or push back against authoritarianism

It doesn't have to be like this. We can refuse to be psychologically manipulated so we are unable to engage in rational thinking and are gripped by fear. We can push back against the authoritarians taking away our freedom and trying to divide us. We can do it the way that all successful social reform movements before us have done it: through actively participating in local, state, and federal government and by engaging in non-violent civil disobedience, if that becomes necessary.

Instead of allowing ourselves to be separated from one another, we can stay connected and meet together in small groups in our homes and neighborhoods. We can develop personal relationships with our elected officials at every level of government—from our local sheriff and elected members of social school boards and city and county councils, to our elected state and federal legislators. If we don't like the way the people we have elected are governing, we can vote them out, or run for office ourselves and help change the laws.

We can talk to the young men and women serving in our community police departments and the U.S. military to remind them of how important it is to protect our human rights and civil liberties, so that if they are ever called upon to implement authoritarian rule, they will make the right choice.

Above all, we can be self-disciplined and make rational decisions that do not lead to violent confrontations, because that kind of behavior only plays into the hands of those, whose ultimate goal is to take away autonomy and more individual freedoms in the United States. During the civil rights movement of the 1950's and 60's, the most profound statements were made by those who sat down in the front of the bus, or in a chair in a segregated restaurant or other public place, and simply refused to move.

Standing our ground during this time of opression and suffering

There are restaurant owners in New York City, who are refusing to follow orders directing them to discriminate against and deny service to the unvaccinated.

There are veteran health care workers on the frontlines caring for patients during the pandemic, who are being fired for supporting informed consent rights, and giving up their careers to stand on principle. Many of them suspect that the next cruel order they will be told to obey is to deny lifesaving medical treatment to unvaccinated patients.

There are corporate CEO's and union leaders, who refuse to bow to political pressure to require rank and file workers to get the vaccine or risk losing their jobs.

There are courageous doctors and scientists who have never spoken out publicly before. They are risking their careers by demanding that mass vaccination policies be backed up by good science. They are challenging the government's narrative that the natural immunity is not as good as vaccine acquired immunity and are criticizing the long-term safety of mRNA vaccines.

There are state lawmakers, who are listening to the people and refusing to vote for the passage of forced vaccination laws that perpetuate the illusion that vaccine passports are the only solution of ending the pandemic.

These Americans are refusing authoritarianism. They are heroes, and they are on the right side of history.

They and many other brave Americans are helping us make our way through this time of fear, oppression and suffering when the cultural values and beliefs that have guaranteed freedom in this great country of ours are being tested.

Restoring the spirit of freedom to the center of our culture

I believe we will come together and pass this test. We will act responsibly to protect our liberty. We will restore the spirit of freedom to its rightful place at the center of our culture.

We will do it because we know if we can tag, track down and force individuals against their will to be injected with biologicals of known and unknown toxicity today, then there will be no limit on which individual freedoms the state can take away in the name of greater good tomorrow.

If individuals are forced against their will to be injected with biologicals of known and unknown toxicity, then there will be no limit by which individual freedoms can be taken away in the name of greater good. You can choose to be a hero. You can choose freedom.

It's your health, your family, your choice. And our mission continues:

No forced vaccination, Not in America.

Chapter 27

Robert F. Kennedy, Jr., New York Times Bestselling Author

In this chapter, I summarized some of what RFK, Jr., reveals in his latest book, "The Real Anthony Fauci." It ranked number one on the NY Times' list of top-selling books.

"In my latest book—'The Real Anthony Fauci: Bill Gates, Big Pharma, and the Global War on Democracy and Public Health'- I take an in-depth look at the disastrous consequences of Dr. Anthony Fauci's 50-year reign as America's public health czar.

As director of the National Institute of Allergy and Infectious Diseases (NIAID), Dr. Anthony Fauci dispensed $6.1 billion in annual taxpayer-provided funding for scientific research.

The research I conducted in my new book exposes how Fauci's yearly disbursements allow him to dictate the subject, content and outcome of scientific health research across the globe.

These annual disbursements also allow Fauci to exercise dictatorial control over the army of "knowledge-and-innovation leaders" who populate the "independent" federal panels that approve and mandate drugs and vaccines—including the committees that allowed the Emergency Use Authorization of COVID-19 vaccines.

Fauci uses the financial clout at his disposal to wield extraordinary influence over hospitals, universities, journals and thousands of influential doctors and scientists—whose careers and institutions he has the power to ruin, advance or reward.

These are the same doctors who appear on network news shows, publish pages of influential media, and craft and defend the pharmaceutical cartel's official narratives.

Instead of addressing the rise in chronic diseases, Fauci transformed NIAID from a world-class regulator into a product incubator for Big Pharma by developing new drugs and vaccines for which he, his agency and his employees often share patents and royalties.

For example, Fauci and four of his hand-selected deputies will partake with Moderna in millions of dollars in royalties from sales of Moderna's COVID vaccine—which was co-developed by Moderna and NIAID.

Fauci has made himself the leading proponent of "agency capture"—the subversion of democracy and public health by the pharmaceutical industry.

As "The Real Anthony Fauci" reveals, Fauci has steadily failed upward. His legacy is a nation that uses increasingly more pharmaceuticals, pays nearly three times more for prescription drugs than people in dozens of other countries, and has worse health outcomes and a sicker population than other wealthy nations.

Today—prescription drugs—many developed by the National Institutes of Health—(NIH) during Fauci's tenure at NIAID—are America's third leading cause of death.

50 Years as the 'J. Edgar Hoover of Public Health'

Fauci has survived half a century in his government post—he's the J. Edgar Hoover of public health—by kowtowing to (and profiting from) pharmaceutical interests.

He launched his career during the early AIDS crisis by partnering with pharmaceutical companies to sabotage safe and effective off-patent therapeutic treatments for AIDS.

The FDA deemed AZT too toxic for human use. Many researchers today argue AZT killed far more people than AIDS.

AZT, at $10,000 per patient last year, became history's most expensive commercial drug—one that made billions for GlaxoSmithKline.

In early 2000, Fauci shook hands with Gates in the library of Gates' $147 million Seattle mansion cementing a partnership that would aim to control and profit by billions, in a global vaccine enterprise with unlimited growth potential.

In 2009, Gates stood before the United Nations and declared the "Decade of Vaccines." He committed $10 billion with the goal of inoculating the entire global population with multiple jabs by 2020.

Through funding leverage and carefully cultivating personnel relationships with heads of state and leading media and social media institutions, the Pharma-Fauci-Gates alliance, exercises dominion over global health policy.

Gates and Fauci now wield far-reaching influence and unprecedented power to shut down the global economy, abolish civil and constitutional rights, impose police state surveillance and engineer the greatest upward shift of global wealth in human history.

In my book I lay bare how Fauci, Gates and their collaborators:

- Invented and weaponized a parade of global pandemics with their enriched Pharma partners and increased the power of public health technocrats and Gates' entourage of international agencies.

- Used "gain-of-function" experiments to breed pandemic superbugs in shoddily constructed, poorly regulated laboratories in Wuhan, China, and elsewhere, under conditions that almost certainly guaranteed the escape of weaponized microbes.

- Teamed with government technocrats, military and intelligence planners, and health officials from the U.S., Europe and China to stage sophisticated pandemic "simulations." Exercises like these, encouraged by the Global Preparedness Monitoring Board and laid the groundwork for imposition of global totalitarianism, including compulsory masking, lockdowns, mass propaganda, and censorship, with the ultimate goal of mandating the coercive vaccination of 7 billion humans.

- Practiced in each of their "simulations," psychological warfare techniques to create chaos, stoke fear, shatter economies, destroy public morale and quash individual self-expression—and then impose autocratic governance.

Stoking COVID-19 pandemic fear

The "Real Anthony Fauci" details how Fauci, Gates and their cohorts used their control of media outlets, scientific journals, key government and quasi-governmental agencies, and influential scientists and physicians to flood the public with fearful propaganda about COVID-19, and to muzzle debate and ruthlessly censor dissent.

Gates and Fauci engaged in almost daily communications throughout the lockdown, and coordinated virtually every decision about COVID-19 countermeasures with each other.

They effectively placed global populations under house arrest, and flooded the mainstream social media with propaganda.

To justify the implementation of draconian measures, they systematically stoked irrational fears and stifled common sense to induce a form of mass psychosis known as "Stockholm Syndrome."

They inspired the belief that total obedience and unquestioning submission to an experimental, shoddily tested, fast-tracked, zero-liability COVID vaccine was their only hope for safe escape from captivity and "return to normal."

As the pandemic unfolded:

- endorsed and exaggerated casualty projections for COVID-19 in order to rationalize draconian lockdowns.

- anointed PCR tests in order to inflate numbers of COVID cases by some 90%.

- facilitated the adoption of new, unprecedented instructions for coroners to attribute COVID as the cause of death "on the death certificate where the disease caused or is assumed to have caused or contributed to death"—with or without a positive COVID-19 test.

- discredited all early COVID-19 treatments like hydroxychloroquine and many other remedies that could have quickly ended the pandemic and saved hundreds of thousands of lives.

Predictably, during the COVID crisis, those policies resulted in the U.S. accounting for 20% of the world's COVID's deaths, despite making up only 4.2% of the global population—another example of Fauci failing upward.

As my book makes clear: Fauci's COVID policies also spawned new insidious authoritarianism—and propelled America down a slippery slope toward a grim future as a dark totalitarian security and surveillance state."

Chapter 28

Florida governor calls for special session to block mask and vaccine mandates

By Mary Villareal — 10/25/21

Florida Governor Ron DeSantis called for a special legislative session on Thursday, October 21, to put a ban on mask and vaccine mandates. The move is in response to the series of mandates imposed by President Joe Biden's administration.

The governor has had enough of the federal government running interference into state business. "We're here to announce that we need to take action to protect Florida jobs," DeSantis said during a news conference at the St. Pete-Clearwater International Airport.

The legislative proposals set by DeSantis include the provision for reemployment assistance for people who were fired due to their failure to comply with an employer's vaccine mandate. A separate proposal seeks to give Floridians compensation if they develop an adverse reaction to the vaccine.

Another proposal seeks that employers who fire their workers solely based on the vaccine mandate would be prohibited from enforcing non-compete agreements against the employees. A provision would require employers to provide religious and health exemptions, and companies that fail to notify their employees about such exemptions would be held liable to lawsuits.

The press conference is the closest that the DeSantis' administration had come up to repudiate vaccine mandates. "The idea that vaccine mandates are needed to create safe workplaces is a complete lie, and it's continued to be repeated and you should know that it's not at all backed up by science. The science says the complete opposite, and that's a fact," Florida's Surgeon General and Secretary of Health Dr. Joseph Lapido said.

DeSantis said: "We have a federal government trying to use the heavy hand of government to force these injections on a lot of folks who believe that decision should be theirs, their freedom of medical choice. Your right to earn a living should not be contingent on getting shots."

He added that it is the people's responsibility to take a stand and fight against the unconstitutional mandates from the federal government.

DeSantis' measures directly oppose Biden's mandates

Biden ordered the Occupational Safety and Health Administration (OSHA) last month to create a rule requiring all private employers with other 100 employees to mandate vaccines or require weekly COVID-19 tests. According to officials, this rule could potentially affect nearly 80 million workers and businesses could face up to $14,000 per violation. (Related: Dallas based Southwest Airlines to ignore State of Texas ban on vaccine mandates, setting up major legal fight.)

The rule is not yet in effect, but a large number of private companies have already mandated vaccines for their employees in anticipation of this rule.

Charles Heekin, an attorney from Charlotte County, said that the Florida Legislature could address the vaccine mandate by building its own right-to-work protection in the state's Constitution.

Currently, Florida is an at-will employment state where employers can fire, demote, hire, promote or discipline their employees for almost any or no reason at all. The strongest way out from vaccine mandates is through legislative action.

DeSantis signed an executive order in April that bans vaccine passports in the state. In May, he signed a bill that codified the ban. The law now prohibits businesses from requiring customers to prove their vaccination status while effectively prohibiting government entities in Florida from issuing such documents.

"In Florida, your personal choice regarding vaccinations will be protected and no business or government entity will be able to deny you services based on your decision," DeSantis said before he signed the bill into law.

Meanwhile, Republicans in Texas, Wyoming and Nebraska are also considering statewide laws against vaccine mandates. A special session in Texas wrapped up on a bill backed up by Governor Greg Abbott that would counter the federal vaccine mandate.

Lawmakers in Wyoming will be holding a special session next week to consider their own bills to block vaccine mandates. In Nebraska, lawmakers still need more votes to trigger a special session to consider similar bills.

Chapter 29

Natural News — November 12, 2021

10 States file lawsuit over "unconstitutional and unlawful" COVID-19 vaccine for healthcare workers

Ten states have taken legal action against the Biden administration's COVID-19 vaccine mandate for healthcare workers that they fear could exacerbate staffing shortages.

A federal court has already temporarily blocked the vaccine mandate for private employers, but a stricter one directed at healthcare workers that does not allow them to opt out of the vaccine. It impacts more than 17 million nurses across 76,000 healthcare facilities and healthcare providers who receive funding from government health programs, among other healthcare workers.

The attorney generals of Missouri, Nebraska and Alaska filed the suit, with the states of Kansas, Iowa, South Dakota, Arkansas, New Hampshire, North Dakota and Wyoming joining the coalition to fight the mandate.

In an official statement, Missouri Attorney General Eric Schmidtt said: "Unfortunately, with the latest mandate from the Biden Administration, last year's healthcare heroes are turning into this year's unemployed."

He called it "unconstitutional and unlawful" and said that it could lead to a healthcare collapse.

One reason the coalition maintains the mandate is unlawful is because the federal government is using it to take away the power that belongs to states. The 58-page file states: "Vaccination requirements are matters that depend on local factors and conditions. Whatever might make sense in New York City, St. Louis or Omaha could be decidedly counterproductive in rural communities like Memphis, Missouri, or McCook, Nebraska."

It adds: Federalism allows states to tailor such matters in the best interests of their communities. The heavy hand of CMS's (Centers for Medicare and Medicaid services) nationwide mandate does not. This Court should set aside that rule as unlawful agency action under the Administrative Procedure Act.

Healthcare worker shortages could get worse thanks to mandate

In addition, the suit argues that the mandate is going to make existing healthcare worker shortages even worse, especially in rural areas in many of the participating states, where some people are especially hesitant.

Many healthcare workers are simply unwilling to get the jab, and some hospital execs have reported that their staff has said they will walk away from their jobs rather than comply with these mandates. The Arkansas Department of Human Services, for example, already has more than 1,000 unfilled positions at its healthcare facilities, and this is expected to get worse once the mandate is in place.

Some healthcare workers are resisting the vaccine on the grounds that they have already recovered from COVID-19 and therefore have some degree of natural immunity. However, the agency that issued the mandate, the Centers for Medicare & Medicaid Service, has said that proof of natural immunity will not be permitted in lieu of a vaccine, citing a study from the CDC about natural immunity that several scientists have challenged. The CDC maintains that people with natural immunity can still benefit from getting the vaccine, and while some health experts agree, many others say that it simply is not necessary in those who have recovered from the virus.

The lawsuit also contends that the requirement is unreasonably broad as it impacts volunteers and staff members who do not interact with patients.

Healthcare facilities that do not comply with the vaccine mandate face penalties such as fines and being excluded from Medicare and Medicaid programs.

The lawsuit comes after similar ones were filed by Republican-led states to challenge the Biden mandate for federal contractors and businesses with more than 100 employees. The mandate does allow those who do not get the jab to agree to wear masks and undergo weekly testing for COVID-19 instead. It takes effect on January 4.

Chapter 30

Published by the National Vaccine Information Center—August 2, 2021

COVID vaccine mandates strongly opposed in Europe, U.S., as vaccine failures increase

Since coronavirus pandemic lockdowns were implemented by many governments in 2020, people around the world have held largely peaceful protests against unprecedented social distancing restrictions that are devastating global economies and ruining people's lives. Now, faced with being ordered to obey new laws that require them to be injected with COVID-19 vaccines in order to enter public spaces or hold a job, on July 24, 2021—World Freedom Day—hundreds of thousands of people of all ages took to the streets in Australia, United Kingdom, France, Italy, Greece and Germany to publicly challenge oppressive public health laws.

The messages on the signs they held were diverse but they were united in pushing back against government overreach. The brave determination of people, in democracies around the world who are publicly defending civil liberties—freedom of thought, speech, conscience and assembly—and the human right to informed consent to medical risk taking, demonstrates that the spirit of freedom lives in the hearts and minds of people everywhere. Both those who gather in the public squares of cities big and small and those who are watching are inspired by this commitment to defending liberty.

In the United States, no large demonstrations have been held yet, but polls reveal the nation is sharply divided about COVID-19 mandates. A Politico/Harvard poll taken in late June 2021 found that Americans were evenly split on whether children should be required to get the COVID-19 vaccine to go to school and more than half of employed Americans are against COVID-19 vaccine requirements for holding a job, while almost 70% of Americans oppose being required to show proof of a COVID-19 vaccination to enter a store or business. A recent CS Mott Children's Hospital poll found that more than half of the parents in the U.S. with children between the ages of three and eleven say it is unlikely they will give their children the COVID-19 vaccine.

AUSTRALIA: "The Lockdown is Killing Us, Not COVID"

With a population of 25 million people, Australians have been subjected to repeated strict lockdowns over the past 18 months and the government's "stay at home" lockdown in early July 2021 was imposed on New South Wales, Victoria and South Australia, where more than half the country's population lives. The 30-day rigid social distancing restrictions were enacted after 176 new daily infections were registered in the whole country.

In response, thousands of Australians gathered in Sydney, Melbourne, and Brisbane on July 24 to protest the lockdown. Social distancing restrictions that have been imposed include compulsory masking in all indoor non-personal residence settings; most schools closed; restrictions on how far people can travel from their homes; no going to work except for designated "essential" employees (who must be tested every three days); exercising and gathering outdoors only in groups of two; shopping only for essential items; attendance at funerals limited to ten people but weddings are banned, and other limits on person-to-person social interaction.

PANDEMIC PANDEMONIUM

In what the U.K. newspaper Daily Mail described as "frenzied crowds" coming together on July 24, there were estimates that as many as 10,000 protesters marched from Victoria Park to Town Hall in the central business district. Carrying signs calling for "freedom" and "the truth" and "I don't consent" and "Wake Up Australia!" and "We are not your slaves" and "unmasked, untested, unvaxxed, unafraid" and "I am not a biohazard" and "Our kids are not your guinea pigs" and "No false tests, no false cases, no lockdowns" one protester said, "We don't give a f*** mate, this lockdown is killing us." Another agreed: "I'm against lockdowns, they're killing my business."

Dozens of protesters climbed onto roofs of a train station and Woolworths store as the crowd gathered around Town Hall singing the Australian national anthem. One observer said on social media, "Protest stretches right down Broadway! Absolutely massive turnout." The Sydney protest was mostly peaceful but when mounted police told the demonstrators to disperse or they would be pepper sprayed, some broke through a police barrier and threw plastic bottles and plants at officers. The New South Wales Police Minister confirmed 57 people were arrested and charged and a "strike force has been established to investigate who was in attendance."

On July 28, the Australian Prime Minister called in military personnel to help enforce social distancing restrictions in Sydney and extended the lockdown for another month after 239 new cases of COVID-19 were detected in the city of five million people within a 24-hour period. Residents will be forced to wear a mask outside their homes and must stay within 3 miles of their homes, only going out for "essential" activities like food shopping.

On July 30, the Australian government used helicopters and the Army to help police enforce its 'Zero COVID' lockdown in Sydney and issue $500 fines for failure to mask. The BBC reported that Australian Defense Force soldiers will begin conducting unarmed patrols of the streets this week. According to media reports, sirens could be heard throughout the city and helicopters blared messages that "this is public health order—do not break rules—you will be found and fined." Road blocks were set up in a military show of force in response to the public demonstrations earlier in the week, although soldiers are under police command. Starting this week, military personnel will accompany police going door to door to ensure that people who have tested positive for COVID-19 are isolating."

Reuters reports that the Australian COVID-19 vaccination rate for adults stands at 18 percent and the Prime Minister has said 80% of adults must get vaccinated before the border, which has been sealed since the pandemic began, will be reopened.

BRITAIN: "No Forced Testing, No Forced Vaccines"

In May 2021, a 12-mile procession of tens of thousands of people ended at Parliament Square in a protest against continuing lockdowns and vaccine passports as a condition of accessing public venues. On July 19, the British government lifted the COVID-19 lockdown that had been in place for over a year, eliminating masking requirements, work from home, and limits of numbers on people who can gather together, which allowed for the full opening of restaurants and other public venues without social distancing restrictions.

Just five days after the lockdown restrictions were lifted, thousands of people made their way to Trafalgar Square on July 24 to signal their opposition to future lockdowns, as well as to protest against the showing of COVID-19 vaccine passports as a condition of entering public spaces. There were banners draped in front of the speaker podium saying, "the public demands live debate" and "science is not science without discussion" and demonstrators held signs that said "No force testing, no forced vaccines" and "We are the lions in a world of sheep" and "If you tolerate this, your children will be next."

Toward the end of the July 24 demonstration, the huge gathering in Trafalgar Square in unison sang, "You'll Never Walk Alone."

The United Kingdom, which has a population of 57 million, ranks in the top 20 most COVID vaccinated nations, with an adult vaccination rate of over 57 percent.

FRANCE: "My Body is Mine" and "It is My Choice"

Paris, France and the cities of Marseille, Montpelier, Nantes and Toulouse saw tens of thousands of people take to the streets on World Freedom Day to protest against a proposed law that would require all health care workers to get COVID-19 vaccinations or lose their jobs. People will be barred from entering restaurants or other public venues, effectively preventing them from participating in public life unless they have a health pass showing proof of COVID-19 vaccination, recovery from the disease or a recent negative COVID-19 test. A care assistant at Strasbourg nursing home expressed her disgust with the proposed law, saying it is "the blackmail of caregivers who were at the front lines during the first wave and who are now threatened with "no more pay" and even being fired.

A huge crowd of over 160,000 people or more, many chanting "freedom, freedom" and carrying signs saying "stop the dictatorship" and "Big Pharma shackles freedom" and "no to the pass of shame" and "vaccines: fake freedom" and "don't touch our children" were met by police deploying tear gas and a water cannon used against some of them. Reuters reported that scuffles broke out at the Champs-Elysees and the Gare Saint-Lazare railway station. The demonstrators met at the Bastille plaza and marched through Eastern Paris and also gathered at Place Trocadero near the Eiffel Tower to protest the required carrying of a "health pass."

Just two days after witnessing several hundred thousand people voicing their opposition to the proposed new public health law, on July 26, the French Parliament voted the pass the law that will take effect this week.

Five days later on July 31, several hundred thousand French citizens of all ages again flooded into the streets of Paris with signs saying "We are not guinea pigs" and "It is our choice" and "My body is mine" and "Health Terror—I will not submit" and the 4th wave is in opposition to the new COVID-19 vaccine and vaccine passport. According the media reports, four marches dovetailed into the Place de la Bastille, with healthcare workers in white coats leading some of them, and were met by waiting squads of gendarmes and CRS riot police with water cannons. Demonstrators also gathered at the Arc de Triomphe at the top of the Champs-Elysees and at the Villiers metro station in northwest Paris.

Reportedly, about 150 protest events also took place in cities around France, which has a population of about 67 million and an estimated COVID vaccination rate of about 47.5 percent or more.

ITALY: Enough Dictatorship: No Green Passes

Thousands of people gathered in Rome, Genova, Milan, Naples, Turin and across the other cities in Italy on July 24 to voice their opposition to the government's imposition of social distancing and COVID-19 vaccine requirements on citizens, including a requirement to carry the "Green Pass," which is an extension of the European Union's digital COVID certificate. The Green Pass will be required to enter cinemas, museums, indoor swimming pools, sports stadiums or eat indoors at restaurants proving that a person has been vaccinated, has had a recent COVID-19 or has recovered from the coronavirus infection.

Chanting and carrying signs that said "Freedom" and "No Green Pass" and "Down with the dictatorship" and "Better to die free than to live like slaves" and "against vaccination obligations" and "government does terrorism" and "shame-shame," reportedly about 80 cities in Italy saw demonstrations on World Freedom Day. These included an estimated nine thousand people in Milan, who marched in procession to the Piazza Duomo, the Galleria Vittoria Emanuele and to the Piazza Scala in front of Town Hall. One banner said "Big Pharma out of the state—no to multinationals."

About five thousand people gathered in Piazza Castello in Turin with signs that said "We want to have freedom to choose—the freedom to go wherever we want without being tied to a sheet." In Rome, where there have been anti-lockdown demonstrations over the past year to protest then closure of cafes, bars and restaurants, an estimated two thousand demonstrated and the police intervened to disperse the crowd with armored vehicles.

Italy has a population of about 60 million people, with nearly 52 percent vaccinated for COVID-19.

GREECE: "Hands Off Our Children"

Thousands of people gathered in Omnia Square in the center of Athens on July 24 to express their opposition to the government's COVID-19 vaccine mandate. They carried signs saying "No mandatory vaccinations" and "No blackmail to dismiss" and "No separation of Greeks" and "Hands off our children." The leader of the anti- COVID vaccine movement in Greece, cardiologist Faidon Vovolis, MD addressed the huge crowd, which according to Athens News, included "not only anti-vaccination activists, but also food and tourism entrepreneurs, clergy, citizens disaffected by the overall government leadership over the pandemic, and vaccinated citizens who view recent government measures as anti-democratic.

Greek police used tear gas and water cannons to disperse the demonstrators who had rallied outside the Parliament building to protest COVID-19 vaccine requirements for workers, such as health care workers. Reuters said that about 45 percent of Greece's 11 million population is already vaccinated.

GERMANY: "For Peace, Freedom, Truth"

Berlin has been the site of several large demonstrations against lockdowns for COVID-19 vaccine passports over the past year. On August 1, 2021, tens of thousands of citizens marched in the streets of Berlin to protest lockdowns that have restricted dining indoors at restaurants or staying in a hotel and requirements to provide proof of COVID vaccination, defying a ban by German lower and upper administrative courts on public demonstrations. Berlin's administrative court had refused to authorize 13 demonstrations, some of which had been organized by the Querdenker (Lateral thinker) anti-lockdown movement.

Berlin's police department deployed more than 2,000 officers armed with batons, pepper spray and water cannons as the crowds made their way from Berlin's Charlottenburg neighborhood, past the Tiergarten park and on the Brandenberg Gate. Reportedly, police in heavily armed vans dragged protesters across roads and into the vans with marchers shouting for freedom and the lifting of mandatory masking and travel bans. Protesters continued to march in the evening through the city streets and 600 people were arrested. Germany has a population of 83 million and 52 percent have been fully vaccinated.

Human rights watch: COVID-19 triggers wave of free speech abuse

On February 22, 2021, Human Rights Watch published a report for an end to excessive restrictions on free speech and peaceful demonstrations where people are criticizing COVID-19 lockdowns, mandatory masking and other social distancing regulations that restrict civil liberties. The Human Rights Organization said:

At least 83 governments worldwide have used the COVID-19 pandemic to justify violating the exercise of free speech and peaceful assembly ...Authorities have attacked, detained, prosecuted, and in some cases killed critics, broken up peaceful protests, closed media outlets, and enacted vague laws criminalizing speech that they claim threatens public health. The victims include journalists, activists, healthcare workers, political opposition groups, and others who have criticized government responses to the coronavirus...Governments and other state authorities should immediately end excessive restrictions on free speech in the name of preventing the spread of COVID-19.

Decentralized government in the U.S. makes a national COVID-19 vaccine mandate more difficult

Unlike centralized governments in Europe and many other parts of the world, the founders of the United States of America ensured in the U.S. Constitution that this country would operate with lawmaking power shared between national, state, and local governments. The fact that lawmaking power in the U.S. does not solely reside with the federal government, which is composed of the legislative (U.S. Congress), Executive (President/federal agencies) and Judicial (federal courts) branches, so far has protected the U.S. population from being subjected to the same kind of uniform lockdown restrictions and now, the same kinds of COVID-19 vaccine mandates that are being implemented in European Union countries and other nations with centralized federal governments.

Since most public health laws in the U.S. fall under the legal jurisdiction of states, if a resident does not like the lockdown, masking, social distancing or COVID-19 vaccine mandates in the state they are living in, they simply can move to different state that does not have the same kind of oppressive public health laws. The reason so far has been that although there have been smaller anti-lockdown and anti-COVID-19 vaccine mandate demonstrations in the U.S. there have not been massive national demonstrations in the U.S. like those taking place in Europe and other parts of the world.

U.S. Government pushes for an 85% COVID-19 vaccination rate

As of July 28, about 60 percent of the U.S. population of 332 million people age 12 and older had received at least one dose of COVID vaccine and reportedly 50 percent, or about 165 million Americans are "fully" vaccinated. As the third largest country in the world, the U.S. has a high COVID-19 vaccination rate compared to other countries, with only 25 countries recording a higher vaccination rate than the U.S.

According to Johns Hopkins University Coronavirus Resource Center, the country with the largest population in the world at 1.5 billion people—China—has a 16 percent COVID vaccination rate; the country with the second largest population in the world at 1.4 billion people—India—has a 7.4 percent COVID vaccination rate; and Russia, with a population of 146 million people, has a 17 percent COVID vaccination rate.

However, U.S. government officials are pushing for an 85 percent COVID vaccination rate in the U.S., even as the former FDA commissioner says that a combination of natural acquired immunity and vaccine acquired immunity is likely rapidly achieving an 85 percent herd immunity rate with the Delta variant in the U.S. population.

Half to two-thirds of Americans oppose punitive COVID-19 vaccine mandates as companies begin to mandate

Even though polls show that one-half to two-thirds of Americans oppose COVID-19 vaccine mandates, depending on the setting, on July 29, the President announced that all federal workers and contractors must show proof of COVID-19 vaccination. The federal government also is urging corporations, local and state government agencies, medical facilities and other institutions to make vaccination a condition of employment.

Some companies, like Google, Facebook, Morgan Stanley, Ascension Health, The Washington Post, Saks Fifth Avenue, Lyft and Uber, Walmart and Disney, have already mandated employees to get COVID-19 shots in order to continue working for the companies. On July 30, Broadway theaters have announced that all members of the audience will be required to show proof of COVID-19 vaccination and must keep a mask on at all times except when eating or drinking.

Opposition grows as CDC admits fully vaccinated persons can get and efficiently transmit COVID-19

After lifting national masking recommendations for COVID vaccinated persons in May 2021 with the assurance that the vaccine was effective in preventing symptomatic SARS-CoV-2 infection, on July 27, CDC officials abruptly reversed course and said that Americans, whether vaccinated or not, should wear a mask outside their homes in certain places. They said they based that policy change on the new information that the COVID-19 vaccines do not reliably prevent infection and transmission of the Delta variant of SARS-CoV-2 and that the viral load in vaccinated persons who get infected is as high as the viral load in unvaccinated persons who get infected.

CDC officials said the new federal indoor masking policy especially applies to adults in "high risk" areas where there are more people being infected with the Delta variant. The masking directive also applies to all unvaccinated children over the age of two, as well as vaccinated children over age 12 attending school, and additionally includes all teachers, school staff and visitors to schools whether vaccinated or not.

The percentage ratio of infected vaccinated to infected unvaccinated persons in Singapore matches that of a recent SARS-CoV-2 outbreak in Massachusetts. On July 30, Associated Press reported that information in CDC documents revealed that 75 percent of the Provincetown outbreak occurred among fully vaccinated individuals. About 80 percent of them experienced COVID-19 symptoms with the most common being cough, sore throat, muscle aches and fever.

U.S. states push back against COVID-19 vaccine mandates

Over the past year, Americans have been taking action at the state and local level to block COVID-19 vaccine mandates. A number of states have passed laws that restrict COVID-19 vaccine mandates for "vaccine passports" that bar people from entering public spaces. Among the states that have passed laws prohibiting COVID-19 vaccine passports or COVID-19 vaccine mandates in some way are Alabama, Alaska, Arkansas, Arizona, Oklahoma, Florida, Idaho, Iowa, Indiana, Kansas, Kentucky, Louisiana, Missouri, Montana, New Hampshire, North Dakota, Ohio, Oklahoma, Tennessee, Texas, and Utah.

On July 29, the Governor of Texas signed an executive order prohibiting state government agencies from mandating COVID-19 vaccine being distributed under Emergency Use Authorization (EUA) and banning public or private entities that receive state funds from denying entry to those who are not vaccinated and, additionally, banning companies, state and local agencies—including school districts—from requiring mask wearing. He said that Texans, "have the individual right and responsibility to decide for themselves and their children whether they will wear masks, open their businesses, and engage in leisure activities."

Governors for several other states also have issued executive orders prohibiting COVID-19 vaccine mandates and some local and state governments, like New York City, and California, have created legal requirements that force state employees to get vaccinated as a condition of keeping their jobs.

On July 26, the nation's largest healthcare worker union, United Healthcare Workers, demonstrated in New York City against employee COVID-19 vaccine mandates. So far, the COVID-19 vaccine mandate as a condition of employment is also opposed by the American Postal Workers Union, Federal Law Enforcement Officers Association, and United Auto Workers."

Chapter 31

LifeSite News

The segregation of the jabbed and unjabbed is the next stage of the tyrannical 'new normal'

The blame game continues against the unvaccinated and it is affecting many lives and relationships.

Protests against vaccination segregation are occurring all over the world.

You are surely well aware of the divide that has cemented itself in society as a result of vaccination segregation. Not all people who chose to take the experimental COVID jab are afraid of the unjabbed, and more than a few are quite critical of the segregation measures that have been implemented.

However, it cannot be ignored that public health officials have done everything they could to drive a fear-based hysteria of the unvaccinated as some sort of disease-peddling class of unclean citizens.

How many times have we heard terms like "pandemic of the unvaccinated?" There is no evidence for this, in fact there is a growing evidence to the contrary. The dreaded Omicron variant—which causes common cold-like symptoms—has been spread around the world by the vaccinated. And more and more regions are finding that COVID-positive vaccinated are filling up death tallies.

The logical conclusion of such a mentality is that those who are unvaccinated should not be around those who are vaccinated. It is a logical conclusion of an illogical premise, however. If considered just for a moment, the insinuation that the vaccinated are not safe around the unvaccinated is like saying that the jab will protect you from the virus, but not from people who may or may not have the virus.

At any rate, reason or rationality are not required in the COVID era. However, sentiments have been echoed to an alarming degree by the man in charge of public health for the province of Ontario.

One doctor has consistently been one of the most egregious disseminators of anti-unvaccinated propaganda in the anglosphere.

A montage that has gone viral (pun intended) presents a collection of the various claims he has made since the summer about the dangers of the unvaccinated walking among us.

In August he said, "The fourth wave is primarily being fueled by the unvaccinated amongst us."

Could you imagine a phrase with more contempt for a fellow citizen? He could have phrased it a number of different ways, but instead he said, "unvaccinated amongst us." Apparently, it is "us" i.e., the double-jabbed, and the "unvaccinated" that is the group of people who walk "amongst us" like zombies who look to eat our brains.

When Canadian Thanksgiving approached in October, he said, "if it's a mixed group of vaccinated and unvaccinated ... I would suggest you keep your masks on ... " It's bad enough to think that families should not show their smiles to one another after almost two years of separation, but the messaging of fear was even worse.

The idea that families should not gather clearly sends the message that individuals should be worried about being around a loved one who has made a different medical choice.

There is no data to suggest this is valid, and it is an absurd and dangerous way to live.

In November, he addressed questions from the media surrounding the issue of fake vaccine passports being used to enter into establishments, which I can attest to as being widespread across the province. He said that any transmission on these settings where the unvaccinated had snuck their way in "had to be because unvaccinated are mixing with vaccinated ..."

That particular press conference took place before Remembrance Day—a day for honoring fallen veterans who died fighting socialists and communists—and he threw more fuel on the unvaccinated fire by saying—we don't want vaccinated and unvaccinated populations mixing ... "

There is a word for this sort of separation of people based on biological considerations; it is called 'apartheid.'

Two days ago, he was at it again, "a basic means of protecting individuals is stopping the mixing of unvaccinated and vaccinated."

It is amazing that the vaccinated class is so scared of the unvaccinated. Such a disbelief in the efficacy of vaccines would usually render someone an "anti-vaxxer," you would think.

This is no laughing matter, as it is having real consequences on the personal lives of many people. I personally know more than a few people who have been unceremoniously cut out of their family traditions because they will not be coerced into taking a jab against their will.

It is having a demoralizing effect on marriages as well, as some couples are divided on the issue, which means they cannot go into public places together like they used to, when one does not have proof of vaccination. In some cases, a spouse will cave to the pressure and take the jab against his or her will, which cannot be good for marital cohesion.

Perhaps what is most sad is the veritable hatred that has risen because of such rhetoric. A screenshot of a text conversation has made the rounds on social media in Ontario—I can attest to its veracity—as I have spoken to the person who posted it—and it is heartbreaking.

At 12-year-old boy who was reportedly told by his peers to kill himself because he "wasn't jabbed" and "will kill others."

Chapter 32

Global Research — December 14, 2021

In an abstract in the Journal Circulation of the American Heart Association (AMA) there is indication that COVID vaccines "dramatically increase heart inflammation in the people that were studies." This led to a substantial increase in the risk of heart complications, like myocarditis and heart attacks.

Twitter put a note on the post by the AMA, stating that it *could* be misleading and the studies could have errors in it. I chose to include it here because it is consistent with so much other research that I have done which basically agrees with this piece.

There is a British cardiologist who is a public health campaigner, a visiting professor, author of several books and writer of articles in newspapers and has a high profile on social media and television. He is also recognized for campaigning on reducing the over-prescribing of medicines. He is also with the U.K.'s National Health Service and a world-renowned expert in the prevention, diagnosis, and management of heart disease.

This doctor appeared on GB News (a free-to-air television and radio news channel in the U.K.) explaining the findings, and while he was doing so, he mentioned another study conducted by another well-known cardiologist, who wished to remain anonymous, that found the same thing.

He stated as follows:

"A few days ago after this was published, somebody from a very prestigious British institution, cardiologist department, a researcher (whistleblower if you like) contacted me to say that the researchers in his department had found something similar within the coronary arteries linked to the vaccine; inflammation from imaging studies around the coronary arteries.

They had a meeting and these researchers have decided that they're not going to publish their findings because they are concerned about losing research money from the drug industry. Now this person was very upset about it and I wanted to share this on GB news today."

What does this say about the current moment our world is living in? Important information is concealed due to the fact it may threaten one's ability to work, leaving the public uninformed. Pharmaceutical companies not only threaten to stop one's funding if findings go against their business interests, but they also refuse to acknowledge science that calls their products into question.

Many of these companies have long had a disregard for ethics and morals. They've even gone so far as to lie about the efficacy and the safety of their products. One PhD, Emeritus Professor from Vancouver School of Economics, wrote a paper 2010 titled "Tough on Crime?—Pfizer and the CIHR." (Canadian Institutes of Health Research). It is accessible through the National Library of Medicine (PubMed). In it he outlines how Pfizer has been a "habitual offender," constantly engaging in illegal and criminal activities. This particular paper points out that from 2002 to 2010, Pfizer has been "assessed $3 billion in criminal convictions, civil penalties and jury awards" and has set records for both criminal fines and total penalties. Keep in mind these numbers have likely risen.

This is concerning, especially given the fact that these companies have big control over academic and medical institutions, as well as medical education.

"The medical profession is being bought by the pharmaceutical industry, not only in terms of the practice of medicine, but also in terms of teaching and research. The academic institutions of this country are allowing themselves to be the paid agents of the pharmaceutical industry. I think it's disgraceful."

Arnold Seymour Relman (1923-2014), Harvard Professor of Medicine and former Editor-in-Chief of the New England Medical Journal

Off-Guardian.org — December 14, 2021

Yesterday, in a statement to Parliament on the U.K.'s planned "vaccine passport," Health Secretary Sajid Javid admitted the NHS Pass would require three shots for you to be "fully vaccinated."

While many of us predicted this would be the case, it is the first time any British politician has actually said it out loud, and in front of Parliament too.

This incredibly cynical "evolving definition" of "fully vaccinated" is not a new phenomenon, and is not isolated to the U.K. either.

Israel changed their definition of "fully vaccinated" to include the booster months ago. New Zealand's ministry of health is "considering" the same as is Australia.

The EU isn't far behind either, with proposals in place to make travel dependent on having a third dose.

The U.S. hasn't formally adopted a new definition yet, but you'd have to be blind not to see the signs. Just yesterday, the LA Times headlined:

"Should the Definition of 'Fully Vaccinated' Be Changed to Include a Booster Shot?"

An article on Kaiser Health News asks the same thing.

Tony Fauci in the Independent is quoted as saying it's only a matter of time before the definition is updated:

"It's going to be a matter of when, not if" getting a booster shot will be considered being "fully vaccinated," Dr. Fauci said.

Opinion pieces are already appearing asking "is it safe to hang out with the unboosted?"

All in all, it seems pretty clear that, by the time 2022 rolls around, most of the Western world will require three shots in order to qualify as "fully vaccinated."

It is also clear that this won't stop at three. Already, just last week, Pfizer was claiming they may need to "move up the timeline" for a fourth vaccine dose.

This change is being blamed on Omicron, with articles warning the "new variant" can "hit" the vaccinated. Fortune reports:

Omicron is making scientists redefine what it means to be 'fully' vaccinated against COVID

So, the third (and maybe fourth) doses are (allegedly) for Omicron... but that model can extend to perpetuity. In order to go five, six or seven, they'll only need to discover "new variants."

It can keep going and going.

But there is good news in all of this, every time the powers-that-shouldn't-be change the rules in the middle of the game, it's a chance to knock people out of their media-induced hypnosis.

There are promising signs that millions of already-vaccinated will reject the booster. We can build on that.

So, tell your single and double jabbed friends, try to open their eyes to the path they are starting down.

They may consider themselves "fully vaccinated," but the government doesn't and probablynever will.

It's time everyone realized they are chasing an intentionally impossible goal that will be pushed back over the horizon, forever.

Chapter 33

By Dr. Paul Craig Roberts, an American author and economist

The "Omicron variant" is being used to create a new wave of public fear and government control over civil liberties and citizens' bodies despite the known fact that the variant is rarely harmful. Hospitals are falsely reported to be full of Omicron patients.

The media stresses that the more or less harmless variant is highly contagious, and are creating fear out of the ease of catching it. People are urged to protect themselves by taking the jab even though it is a known fact that the Omicron variant is immune to the "vaccine."

Acquaint yourself with the facts:

In Scotland for August and November 2021 over 85% of deaths were in the vaccinated. Boosters are merely boosting COVID infections. Some 40,000 deaths have occurred in the USA, U.K. and EU following vaccination but Omicron is mild. The U.K. Government has manipulated the data to blame the unvaccinated but the vaccinated are at greatest risk.

It was clear from the first cases in South Africa and now in the U.K. and EU that the new Omicron variant of the Coronavirus results in mild disease and very few deaths [not from COVID but] "with COVID." Indeed, South African experts have advised stopping stop-and-trace and quarantining because most of the infected have no symptoms.

More evidence of the failure of vaccines in the face of new infections comes from the U.S. where one of the largest U.S. outbreaks of the new Omicron variant to date is believed to have occurred at Cornell University in Ithaca, New York, where almost all 930 cases over the past week are believed to be of the variant.

All of the confirmed Omicron cases in the Cornell University are among people who are fully vaccinated, and some of them are in people who've also had the booster.

The booster is of course more of the same in the hope that the third dose will do what the first two doses were supposed to do! And the new variant, "Omicron"?

Most of the Omicron cases in the United States have been among the vaccinated, the Centers or Disease Control and Prevention (CDC) said in an update on Friday 10/12/21. Most patients have experienced mild symptoms.

When the media of the entire Western World lends itself to blatant lies in order to boost Big Pharma profits and enhance governments' destruction of civil liberty, the Western World is lost. It is the corrupt Western media that has conspired with governments to destroy freedom in the Western world to the point that all evidence proves beyond any question that the virus has a very low death rate and is easily cured and prevented with CHQ and Ivermectin.

Western peoples need to understand that it is not necessarily Russia and China who are their enemies, but perhaps their own governments and public health officials who are the enemies of mankind".

Chapter 34

Mattias Demet, PhD—Psychotherapist and Professor at Ghent University in Belgium, became widely known as a corona skeptic. He has conducted many interviews some of which can be found on Google. In part this is one of them:

Q. Is there data that the psychological suffering of the population is increasing due to the corona crisis?

These data are still largely missing because agencies that provide it work with significant delays. Nevertheless, the indicators, such as the number of registrations with psychologists, suggest that psychological suffering is increasing. In fact, given the current social context, this makes sense. Where the first lockdown was still experienced as a welcomed shelter in the much too rushed life, we now see that teleworking and the imposed social distance is generating frustration. The lack of social contact in the workplace and elsewhere is beginning to weigh on the mental experience of many people.

Q. In previous interventions, you defended the theory that fear can lead to mass formation under certain circumstances.

What I have said is that the coronavirus has redrawn the fear landscape that already existed. So, there was already a lot of fear in society before the corona outbreak. There has always been fear, but in recent centuries fear has become more and more disconnected. For example, in the Middle Ages, fear was linked to certain objects such as the feudal ruler, hell, eternal damnation and so on. With enlightenment, the medieval view of man and the world was replaced by a scientific ideology. When a story comes along that identifies a clear object of fear like the coronavirus, it can have a huge impact in what I sometimes call "the landscape of fear."

Q. Is fear an inescapable companion of man? Is he permanently looking for a way to position himself in the face of the fear experienced?

From birth, a child tries to form a bond with the other. It fixes on the face of the mother, observes it and imitates it. One question is ubiquitous in this process: What do I have to do to be liked by you? What do I have to do to mean something to you? What touches you? The same questions will come up later in relationships with siblings, schoolmates, teachers, colleagues and all other encounters. We can never know for sure who we should be for the other person, and therefore there is always a fear of falling short. We feel quite comfortable when we are accepted and liked by the other person. Yet the question of how we should relate to the other is always good, for it forces us to change. This is the ultimate sign of maturity and humanity in man.

Q. Does a person find inner peace only when he has the feeling of being accepted?

Initially, we are almost completely captivated by what that one specific other—our primary care people for example—tell us. From countless encounters with other people, we gradually instill some basic principles that generally holds true when it comes to accommodating other people's desires. They serve as a kind of guideline for our actions in social life; in relationships with other people. As the basics become clearer, our dependence on others diminishes. In this way we can steer our own course without having to constantly adapt to what others ask or expect from us. This is how we develop spine and personality. This happens when an individual, or a group of people, develop the ability to resist the dictates and social pressure of a large group. If they can stay true to their basic tenets and refuse to agree with what the larger group, or society, is trying to impose on them they can create a different voice that goes against the voice and story of the masses. If nobody does this anymore, or if too few do it, the French philosopher Michel Foucault argues, society cannot survive. The ability to live and speak in principle, and not to go along with the imposed delusions of the day, is crucial; the courage to say in public what one feels to be true.

The ancient Greeks regarded bold speech as a vital civic virtue. It is a form of truth-telling that opposes rhetoric. The rhetorician tries to convince the listener of a story he himself does not believe in; for strategic reasons he tries to convince the other of something which he himself knows is not true. This is exactly what the word totalitarianism refers to—the arising of the illusion that one story is totally correct. And because one considers the story to be completely correct, one can also realize the story is crossing all ethical boundaries.

I think we notice this dangerous tendency within the dominant corona story: If we want to prevent the ICU's from filling up, we must go into lockdown and shut down the entire society, forbid the elderly to see their grandchildren, we can no longer use first aid administering in the event of an accident. Women who have just given birth are no longer allowed to hold their newborn babies, protests are no longer allowed, people without a vaccine are no longer allowed to travel, etc. If someone had presented such an argument just a few years ago, one would have wondered pityingly about his mental health. Now it seems to be an unshakable truth to many.

Once one has accepted this premise of logic, everything else inevitably flows from it. Every logical counter-argument is systematically pushed out of the field and rendered "harmless" and step-by step all normal ethical boundaries are violated. This kind of logic takes over a society unnoticed, but it is potentially extremely dangerous. History has shown that very clearly. If we want to realize the ultimate goal of history—the creation of the super race—then we have to eliminate all peasants, the handicapped and the Jews. People think that this cannot be compared to what is happening now because at the same time it is considered 'logical' that people who refuse the corona vaccine would hardly be able to participate in social life and also lose their jobs. This again shows how strong the psychological processes are at play.

Q. In your approach, which in a number of ways is inspired by Hannah Ardent's view that fear from mass formation leads to totalitarianism, you pointed to the existing fear that was already circulating in our society before the corona pandemic. To what extent do you think government communication regarding the corona pandemic has brought new fear into our society?

I never really emphasized that myself, but in the meantime, it is clear that this has happened. In Germany, and the United Kingdom, experts admitted that they were fueling fears among citizens to force them to follow the measures more closely. Some regretted that there was something totalitarian about their performance. In Belgium it was no different. It was recently said in a news article, that Belgian experts deliberately worried the population. However, we should applaud the fact that experts are starting to admit this. Some say they have gone too far in their actions, and express their regret. Which is good. Whenever honesty and humanity show itself, we should be grateful for it and not react with resentment.

Q. The Swedish Government had communicated openly about the corona virus with its population from the start; what citizens could do to protect themselves and others. At the same time, it placed a great deal of responsibility and autonomy on the citizens, without correcting them by means of coercive measures, such as very high fines or police interventions. What does the choice to use fear say about the way administrators see the population?

This definitely indicates a serious problem. One always has to choose between two ways of dealing with the population and tackling social problems: either one focuses on power and control, or on good human relations with the population. The latter is based on the belief that if people talk to each other in a casual, sincere and open way, they will find a solution in which the various parties involved feel that their problems are taken into account.

In practice it means that when one imposes one's own vision and preferences on society, through control and power they try to convince you that things will go wrong if the population, or part of the population, does not follow. They try, in other words, to control and manipulate public opinion. In some cases, this develops into the indoctrination and propaganda of totalitarian systems, supplemented if necessary, with terror to radically silence dissident voices.

Sometimes a government uses power, sometimes it instills fear. We should not be too fanatical or too naive about this, but it should be the exception and not the rule and never be the basis of any policy. If one resolutely opts for the fear model, one runs the risk of slipping into what Aristotle called the tyranny of the majority. A democracy is not merely a form of society in which the majority decides. It is a form of society in which the majority decides, but always grants fundamental rights to minorities, such as freedom of expression, self-determination, freedom of ideology and belief. If not, then the majority becomes a tyrant.

Q. Does the behavior of the mass media influence the formation of the masses?

Without mass media, or other well-developed means of propaganda, a totalitarian regime is not possible. Totalitarianism, is radically intolerant of dissident voices. Not only because they break through the unity of thinking, but because they threaten to confront the masses. The dissenting voice usually generates strong aversion.

The dissenters are also an ideal scapegoat for everything that goes wrong. The masses take out all their pent-up frustration and anger on the dissenters. There are quite a few examples of this. Just think of the Crusades, or the French Revolution.

The spokesmen of the masses, the so-called "drivers" of the masses, are allowed to misrepresent things, not be held accountable. In fact, they are allowed to lie, cheat and manipulate because it is assumed that the dominant voice always speaks for the benefit of the collective. "They're doing it for our own good" is a clincher that rings in every crowd. What one forgets is that no one can be sure of what is right, so everyone should always exercise caution and never jettison certain fundamental principles in following "what is good."

We see things seriously going wrong on that point. In practice, the government and the media try to create the illusion that there is a unity of thinking regarding the danger of the coronavirus and take whatever measures needed to combat it within the scientific world. In Belgium it is made clear to doctors that those who dare to cast doubt on the effectiveness of the vaccine risk severe sanctions, even dismissal. In the Netherlands, doctors who prescribe certain drugs for the treatment of COVID can be fined up to 150,000 euros. Dissident voices, researchers and professors are ridiculed and censored. In general, we must say that the repression and censorship of the government and media do not belong in a democracy.

Q. Do you have the impression that the academic world, where an open debate should be the engine of progress, has also found itself in a Pensee Unique (thinking like everyone else)?

For example, my university explicitly grants me the right to freedom of expression. That is only normal because it concerns basic right. I am also sincerely grateful for it. If people respect your basic rights, that's quite something. But I speak on my own behalf, not on behalf of any institution.

Yet there is considerable social pressure on me. At least that's how it feels. And some do not fail to express contempt. This social pressure is also the reason why other academics with dissident views are often silent. If one were to investigate the percentage of academics who voiced critical opinions during the corona virus, one would probably arrive at a very limited amount. Some academics think critically but do not dare to speak critically! Still some others do not think critically and go along globally with the dominant narrative.

Q. Is accepting a story under (peer) pressure a kind of coping mechanism to allay one's fear of not being liked and being rejected by others?

Man is a being that constantly struggles with uncertainty and division and as such, is constantly looking for certainty in stories that put forward clear explanations and solutions. People often realize that these stories are not entirely correct, but they prefer to look away. We see this constantly during the corona crisis. We must trust the government, experts and others such as the pharmaceutical industry, unconditionally. Dissidents threaten the clarity and unity of what people yearn for in crisis situations. 'Anyone who thinks differently is a danger.'

Q. Does the dominant narrative influence the way scientific data is interpreted?

Figures are constructed and interpreted from and on the basis of stories. For example, many doctors and researchers question the mortality rates, which were initially used as an indication of the danger of the virus. According to some doctors, many people died of other conditions while they were registered as corona deaths. Yet that does not get through and people do not seem really able to put the figures into perspective in this way.

Similarly, a German pulmonologist reported that the mortality of severely ill COVID patients in the ICU fell by 50% when aggressive ventilation methods were no longer used. What did those people die from, the virus or the treatment? That is a good question. But it is rarely asked and you will not see the numbers and statistics based on this information.

That shows us the power of the dominant narrative and its impact on the numbers.

Q. Is the population developing new civic virtues as an effect of the intense fear of the coronavirus, and the measures imposed? Does not being able to publicly question, even with scientific evidence provided and the measures it has taken, make for extremely docile and obedient citizens? Is conformism lurking around the corner?

That danger certainly exists. Again, we are touching on a core feature of totalitarianism. In a totalitarian society, the individual effaces himself in an extreme way for the collective. On the one hand, this is demanded by the totalitarian leaders. It arises spontaneously in a crowd. This happened very quickly during the outbreak of the corona pandemic. For example, there was pressure from citizens to unconditionally accept and endorse the measures. A new kind of 'civility' was indeed emerging. Those who doubted or did not comply with the measures were sometimes denounced or reported. And even more interesting was that it had already increased before the corona crisis. In other words, the corona crisis does not stand alone. It fits into a continuous historical process. That process leads straight to a society in which the government controls just about everything.

Unity thinking and mass formation serve as symptomatic solutions to a generalized fear. In fact, we need to find a solution to the underlying social problems that have led to the disproportionate response of the corona crisis. This requires a broad, critical analysis of our current and human world view; the world view of enlightenment. In 1951 Hannah Arendt foresaw that a new totalitarian regime would emerge, one that would no longer be led by gang leaders like Stalin or Hitler, but by dull technocrats and bureaucrats.

Q. Can you paint a picture of what such a totalitarian state might look like?

Totalitarianism is characterized by the government's enormous grip on public space and private space. The Chinese system, in which citizens are awarded points based on their behavior is moving in that direction. Citizens with too few points can no longer travel freely, are denied access to a night life and educational grants pass them by.

A policy of such characteristics can certainly spill over here. A digital corona passport can be a major step in that direction. In the U.K. where such a passport has been in existence since the end of May, it was found that the app connected to it provided much more data than whether or not someone has been vaccinated or not. For example, a whole series of personal data (number plate, employer, biometric and genetic information, convictions) and other medical data would be viewed. Perhaps this is said to be done with good intentions, but good intentions can also be dangerous and lead to dehumanization. It shows that boundaries are blurring. That does not alter the fact that I believe there will be a group that will not go along with that trend so as to prevent this system from closing completely. But it won't be easy. In any case, we will need a lot of perseverance in practicing the virtue of speaking boldly.

Chapter 35

Reality vs. Illusion. People have been robbed of their ability to decipher between fact and fiction

By Dustin Broadbery, writer and researcher

CIA Director, William Casey is reported to have said to Ronald Reagan, "We'll know our disinformation is complete when everything the American people believes is false."

Fast forward thirty years, and there's no piece of fiction the masses will not swallow.

From COVID to the war in the Ukraine, people no longer make their own ideological pilgrimages to the truth—the truth is served oven-ready by their political betters.

Nowadays, there's little distinction between the two hemispheres: reality and illusion. It's not so much that people have been robbed of their ability to decipher between these two, it's that facts have been reoriented into fiction and fiction into facts. It's a degradation of epistemology so momentous, that people don't even know that they don't know what's happening, to quote one former anarchist.

In the grand scheme of things, humanity has perjured themselves and life as we know it has morphed into a sort of science-fiction soap-opera, with a few common ancestors sharing the same reality. Even right-thinking folks require the equivalent of a cerebral chainsaw to hollow out the slew of implausible narratives into something remotely resembling reality. It goes beyond fiction to predictive programming. They're not just deceiving you; they're showing you that they are deceiving you.

What is neither here nor there to the deceived is the track record of their deceivers. The entire fiasco holds water because what people think they know for sure, that just ain't so, is a consensus. A preponderance of fabrications, falsehoods and false prophets governs the spiritual milieu. People worship the prosaic and glorify artifice. Our moral choices are guided by platitude and not virtue, anecdote and not evidence.

There's a war raging alright, but you will find its theatre of operations inside the human psyche. It's a war on consciousness, an atrophy of culture and its stark consequences is the spiritual malaise of humanity.

Then as now, it's not enough for some people to hold a monopoly over knowledge, they must deprive everyone else of its illumination, or go one further to spread ignorance. It goes beyond censoring counter arguments to fomenting falsehoods, it's not so much societal breakdown but self-immolation. People are being misinformed and stupefied and sent out as agents of disinformation to further deconstruct what's left of an already deconstructed reality.

To make matters worse, precisely zero lessons have been learned these past two years. People flounder from one crisis to the next. Walk aimlessly from quarantine camp to air-raid shelter into whichever direction their political higher-ups point them, to deride whoever is nominated as the scourge of society, de jour. The great national pastime is to gather at the pillories and hurl cabbages at anti-vaxxers.

The infowar

If all this sounds remarkably like an info war, then it probably is.

The battle for hearts and minds has moved online. Our divine spark of life is being overhauled to data. Something of divine proportions compels us to the internet, to data—our daily bread (and circuses), our digital avatars living richer, more meaningful lives than their truant owners.

It doesn't matter which side of the fence you're on—a card carrying member of the great awakening on the lockdown left, you're still part of the same problem. You have been taken hostage by a series of narratives laid on with a shovel by the predator class or designed for the sole purpose of keeping you rapt and not informed, sedentary and not spirited. In the world of algorithims everyone is created equal, and data is just data, there's no mortality to it.

These events play out as a nail-biting whodunnit, but the reality is, they're not supposed to be solved. There's no answers nor restitution; it's your attention and not your belief systems which is being harvested.

What these hellhounds want is for you to pick your side, choose your battle, but make sure your battle lines are social media.

According to Voltaire, because those who can make you believe in absurdities, can make you commit atrocities.

If a person's psyche is under siege and they don't designate an enemy to scapegoat, they might get wise to who's really attacking them, and that simply wouldn't do.

In this theatre of the absurd people acclimatize to fiction because it's easier than confronting uncomfortable truths. But under these fertile conditions any version of reality, no matter how precarious, will wash. That's where the great reset enters the fray.

Once you desecrate a person's moralistic and cultural maps of the world, their place in it becomes increasingly untenable. People lose touch with reality and what it means to be human. The ensuing crisis of identity leaves them susceptible to hostile takeover. Amongst other things that could possibly go wrong is the eventual microchipping of the population and brain machine interfaces.

Predictive programming

But there are even stranger things brewing. Predictive programming is the theory of a hidden hand operating the levers of reality. A sort of reality adjustment bureau obfuscating real world events through film, literature and media manipulation. The fundamental principle here is psychological conditioning that reduces people's resistance to the acceptance of planned future events and encourages them to swap concrete reality structures for static constructs, until eventually, our inherited world view is replaced by mythos and archetypes.

That we are living through the objectification of the predator class is no moot point. That's their messiah complex imprinted onto the collective consciousness and projected back onto the real world. By their own volition, the masses are breathing life into these grotesqueries and blotting the social fabric.

Revelation of the method

But it runs even deeper than predictive programming. Some call this Revelation of the Method.

According to Michael Hoffman: first they suppress the counterargument, and when the most opportune time arrives, they reveal aspects of what's really happened, but in a limited hangout sort of way.

We were told the vaccines were harmless until Pfizer rebased their own safety claims, but not before the entire world had been vaccinated. Lockdown apologists across the corporate media are now almost unanimous that lockdowns do more harm than good. This is no arbitrary volte-face, but rather a carefully planned sequence of disclosures when the time is ripe.

It has been suggested that the ruling elite are giving notice of their supremacy. Declaring themselves virtuoso criminal masterminds, who are above the law and beyond reproach. But most of all, they are telling you, in no uncertain terms, that you are without recourse, these events are beyond your control, as is your own destiny for that matter. Eventually a sense of apathy and abulia engulfs humanity, demoralizing to the point of conceding defeat to a system we are powerless to change.

Not that you would have restitution. The house is not designed to do its own housekeeping. Buried deep within their rule of law, is a hidden constitution that states: nothing happens without your consent. In this version of contract law, once the truth is hidden in plain sight, you have agreed to it. There exists someplace an unsigned contract with your unsworn oath on it.

In the end, we're all victims of the same masterstroke, whether keyboard evangelist or state-apologist, everyone is being royally screwed and it's not so much they're laughing at you, it's that you're laughing at yourself.

Aside from COVID-19, Dustin writes about the intelligence state, big tech surveillance, big philanthropy, the co-option of activism and human rights.

You can find his work at https://www.thecogent.org. Or follow him on twitter @ The Cogent1

Chapter 36

I will end this last chapter with the following news piece which was sent to me by a friend dated May 25, 2022. Personally, I've always taken a liking to Florida's Governor Ron DeSantis because he has done so much to make Florida such a livable state while the rest of the nation endured and suffered through this "unlivable" crisis. He was able to defy our political system because he believed as I, and so many others do, that our nation's politics and politicians need some serious change.

To give you an idea of how he chooses to steadfastly buck the system, in an article by Dr. Meryl Nass, dated October 26, 2021, she quotes DeSantis as follows: "Governor DeSantis says that if people are forced by their employer to be vaccinated, and then become ill, the employer will be liable for damages."

Here is the piece of which I speak:

DeSantis Says 'No Way' Will Florida Defer to WHO on Future Pandemics

Florida Governor Ron DeSantis made it clear on Tuesday that his State would not go along with a President Joe Biden decision to defer to the World Health Organization on policies regarding future pandemics.

"We in Florida, there is no way we will ever support this WHO thing. That's not going to happen. No Way," DeSantis said when he heard about the plan.

"You saw a lot of these elites advocate very pernicious policies...part of the reason people want to move here is because we rejected those policies, but they advocated very pernicious policies, including locking kids out of school," he continued.

Florida bucked most of the rest of the country by keeping schools and businesses open during the beginning months of the pandemic when others kept them shut down for months, which led to a migration there from other, more restrictive States.

Former Governor Jeb Bush commented that DeSantis "allowed individuals to determine their own risk tolerance" and lauded that approach.

"His approach works. It's the one that's allowed Florida to emerge from the pandemic as a national model of personal freedom, economic growth, environmental protection, and education excellence," he continued.

"Florida continues to see record population growth, unemployment remains below the national average, the private sector is growing, and Florida remains a national leader in school choice," Bush went on.

Not only that, but Florida did not fare any worse than other populace states in terms of deaths from the virus and its hospitals were not overwhelmed.

Seems like Florida, rather than WHO, should be setting policies for the country since that state's policies actually worked.

WHO was widely criticized by advocating continued shutdowns and restrictions, as well as trying to divert attention away from the likelihood that COVID-19 came from a Wuhan lab in China.

Not only that, but it is a UN-backed, international organization, and should not be making policy for the U.S.

Completely unsurprising is that Biden doesn't see it that way, though. Seems like DeSantis is going to have even more of a migration on his hands if there's another pandemic anytime soon.

EPILOGUE

I have chosen to write this book not because I believe it will change anything, least of all the minds of those who are conditioned to believe that which they are told to believe. However, what I find disturbing, is when I see people's most basic rights violated. This book was written to help us understand the catastrophic consequences when human rights, self-independence, informed consent, and freedom of choice are violated. If such deceit is allowed to continue there will be no end to tracking, tracing and violation of rights.

My main objective here was to search outside the mainstream media for information. To me it is remarkable how much reliable information can be found when one chooses to look beyond the constant and mundane reporting by the same everyday media favorites.

According to the research I did in preparation for this book, I found that the media, i.e. TV, newspapers, magazines and the owners of social media have appointed themselves to be the sole source of information concerning this pandemic and highly experienced and credentialed doctors and experts in their fields have been silenced by censorship. Yet so much dissenting information is labeled "misinformation" and "dangerous lies."

The media refers to those individuals who have not been vaccinated as "anti-vaxxers," "vaccine deniers," "vaccine resisters," and even "murderers" as being the ones prolonging the pandemic.

These attacks on free speech and free choice is daunting at best and terrifying at worst. This massive control through one-sided reporting has gotten so slanted that it would seem impossible to change. But logic tells us that if we refuse to accept all that we are being told on a massive level, we can defeat those outside forces whose only aim is to gain more money and more power and to reduce ours. Logic tells us also that there is strength in numbers. In fact, I see it happening already. Each day I see more and more people beginning to understand what is happening and the tide is turning.

I believe in the end it will all turn out okay if we can learn to apply greater faith in ourselves and withdraw our faith in those whose only objective is to instill fear and make us weaker, more vulnerable and therefore, more controllable.

Sources

Bitchute

Brighteon.com

Brighteon.tv

Children's Health Defense (RFK, Jr.)

Global Research.ca

Google

Herald Trubune.com

LifeSite News

National Vaccine Information Center—Your Health. Your Family. Your Choice

Naturalnews.com

Newstarget -Uncensored and Independent Media News

Off Guardian.org

One America News (OAN)

The Epoch Times.com

USNews.com

VaccineNews.com

About the Author

Myrna Skoller was born and raised in New York and her home is in South Florida. She has previously written five other books, "Miracle on 81st Street" "Private Lessons with Jesus" "Letters to Heaven and Back" and two children's books, "I Remember Grandpa" and "Sydney Goes to Bat."

CPSIA information can be obtained
at www.ICGtesting.com
Printed in the USA
BVHW030401270822
645604BV00016B/1532